Christian Values

Edited by
Edward Stourton and Frances Gumley

Hodder & Stoughton
LONDON SYDNEY AUCKLAND

Copyright © 1996 by Helena Kennedy,
Michael Fogarty, Hugo Young, John Patten, Philip Dowson
Stuart Horner, John Tavener and Edward Heath

First published in Great Britain 1996

1 3 5 7 9 10 8 6 4 2

British Library Cataloguing in Publication Data
A record for this book is available from the British Library

ISBN 0 340 64272 6

Typeset by Hewer Text Composition Services, Edinburgh
Printed and bound in Great Britain by
Cox & Wyman Ltd, Reading, Berks

Hodder and Stoughton Ltd
A Division of Hodder Headlines PLC
338 Euston Road
London NW1 3BH

Contents

Foreword

The celebrations marking the Centenary of the foundation of Westminster Cathedral have given a unique opportunity to further the vision of its founder, Cardinal Herbert Vaughan. He was anxious that the Cathedral should be a sign and symbol of the presence of Jesus Christ in the City and in the nation. Through its liturgy and music, its pastoral work and stunning architecture, that vision is being fulfilled.

The series of Centenary lectures arranged as part of the celebration are here made available to a wider public. Together with the concerts, exhibition, pilgrimages and liturgies which marked the Centenary, they seek to contribute towards that 'Civilisation of Love' which Pope Paul VI spoke of in 1975.

Mgr George Stack
Administrator

Introduction

Nothing provokes shuffling in the pews like a sermon on the obligation to carry faith into the world of work. When a priest reminds his congregation that the creed they say on Sunday morning should influence the way they behave in their professional lives on Monday morning there is a chorus of blown noses, cleared throats and whispered admonitions to restless children. The phenomenon is especially marked in prosperous metropolitan parishes where people hold the sorts of job that give them a real influence over the lives of others. Most of us would much rather not be reminded of this disagreeable duty; it is easier to keep religion in its box, in the arena of personal conduct. How many of us would stand up at a board meeting, an editorial conference or a political debate and argue a point on the basis of Catholic teaching?

The value of these essays is that they try to build the bridge between the world of church and the world of work. Not all the authors are Catholic, but all have thought hard about the way to make judgments on secular issues from a Christian standpoint. And all of them have held or do hold positions that mean their judgments matter to the rest of us.

Their conclusions are far from orthodox, and many of them will make awkward reading for our bishops. Hugo Young's picture of a world 'where Rupert Murdoch is widely confused with God' is grim enough to make any journalist ashamed, but he is equally critical of what he describes as the 'authoritarian, defensive, anti-truth' mentality of some parts of the Church. Helena Kennedy argues forcefully against 'the declared inclusion of Christian values in the law in contemporary society'. And John Patten berates the clergy for failing to understand and preach the moral virtues of capitalism.

The essays are full of surprises. I must confess to some trepidation when I saw Michael Fogarty's subject: 'Christian Values in the Economy'; in the event he has made the moral dimension of the dismal science transparent and compelling. Sir Philip Dowson talks about something much more engaging than church and cathedral architecture; his essay is an education in the way to look at bricks and mortar – and indeed concrete and steel – in moral terms. In the same way John Tavener speaks about far more than music – weaving an inspiring and compelling argument about spirituality and art which touches people in a way which is unusual today.

Dr Stuart Horner addresses the very current concern about Christian ethics and medical progress by reclaiming purloined historical territory. And Sir Edward Heath brushes aside any temptation he may have felt to dwell on the many peccadilloes of his colleagues – which have consumed so much newspaper ink during recent months – giving us an altogether grander political 'tour d'horizon'.

It is greatly to the credit of the Church hierachy that it sponsored this series which so often questions the Church's official position, and it suggests a certain confidence in the Catholic faith's ability to compete in what Helena Kennedy refers to as the 'market-place of ideas'.

That confidence is all the more remarkable in the light of the intellectual climate of the time when Westminster Cathedral was built a century ago.

Although formal Christianity may have had a much closer hold over the lives of ordinary people then than it does today, the élites in the worlds of science, philosophy

Introduction

and politics were already well advanced along roads which seemed destined to end with the destruction of religion. Karl Marx had produced a historical formula of such force that many people felt its logic was unanswerable. Frederich Nietzsche had pronounced God dead and begun the search for a morality 'beyond Good and Evil'. And Charles Darwin had challenged God's place in creation through empirical observation.

There must have been those who doubted whether the Cathedral would survive a hundred years as a living place of worship; that intellectual inheritance might have been expected to turn the building into a historical curio, preserved only for the evidence it carried of habits of mind which had outlived their value or credibility.

Instead the centenary reaffirmed the Cathedral's place at the centre of national life; the writers emerge from these essays as acutely conscious of the pluralism of their society and the challenges to Christianity thrown up by the intellectual upheavals of the twentieth century. But at the same time all seem convinced of the truth their faith can offer.

These essays were originally a series of talks given in connection with the Cathedral's centenary and thanks are due to Westminster Theatre for providing a forum where the talks could come alive. Equally we owe thanks to Eric Major for editing them in a way that ensures they stay alive on the page.

Edward Stourton

Helena Kennedy QC

Chancellor of Oxford Brookes University

Helena Kennedy QC was born in 1950, called to the Bar in 1972 and became Queen's Counsel in 1991. She was made an Honorary Doctor of Law by the following: University of Strathclyde 1992; University of Teesside 1993; Keele University 1994; Lancaster University 1994 and Leeds Metropolitan University 1995.

She practises predominantly in criminal law, undertaking leading work of all kinds, but also engages in judicial review, public enquiries and sex discrimination work. One of the many prominent cases of the last decade in which she has acted was the Guildford Four Appeal.

A frequent broadcaster and journalist on law and women's rights, she was a contributor to *The Bar on Trial* 1982, *Child Sexual Abuse Within the Family* 1985, and *Balancing Acts* 1989. She created the BBC TV series *Blind Justice* 1987 and, among many other programmes, presented the BBC's *Heart of the Matter* throughout 1987, *Raw Deal on Medical Negligence* in 1989, *The Trial of Lady Chatterley's Lover* 1990 and *Time Gentleman, Please* for BBC Scotland 1994. She was the first female moderator of television *Hypotheticals*.

Her book *Eve was Framed*, on women and the criminal justice system, was published in 1992 and the same year she received the Women's Network Award for her work for women and justice. In 1993 she was guest speaker at the Women of Distinction Luncheon and at the International Conference of Women Judges held in New Zealand.

Her other extensive activities include the Chair of Charter '88 and of the Standing Committee for Youth Justice; Council Member of the Howard League for Penal Reform; and she chairs the Committee on Widening Participation for the Further Education Funding Council.

1

Helena Kennedy QC
Christian Values in the Law

The legal system is now coming under greater scrutiny than ever before, partly because of concern about crime and punishment, in what is perceived to be a more disorderly society, and partly because public confidence has been shaken by the recent miscarriages of justice. What values should be embodied in the law? Can we ever talk of Christian values in the law when we live in a multi-religious society? Are demands for retribution consistent with Christian practices? Is the current discourse on individual rights a derogation of our responsibilities to other human beings?

1

It seems a particularly opportune time for us to consider the values or absence of values in our contemporary world. Lord Nolan has been presiding over a committee called into being to examine ethical standards in public life because there was such public alarm about the behaviour of those who seemed to be abusing positions in public life for their own financial gain: MPs asking questions in the House on behalf of professional lobbyists if the price was right, newly retired government ministers sliding into incredibly highly paid jobs in the very industries which they had privatised, the creation of an unprecedented number of quangos – one for every ten thousand of the population, spending one third of the total public expenditure budget – with thousands of paid appointments going to the friends of those in power, with no public accountability.

We have also had the exposure of appalling boardroom greed. Wherever I go I meet people who despairingly and plaintively ask, 'Whatever happened to the public service ethic?' and 'What has happened to the idea of service to one's fellow citizens for its own sake rather than for the maximum personal benefits that can accrue?' Perhaps that idea was abandoned at the same time that one of our political leaders decided there was no such thing as society.

Lord Nolan's investigation came hard on the heels of the Scott Inquiry, which arose from the scandalous Matrix Churchill affair where three industrialists were put on trial for selling weapon components to Iraq in breach of a government embargo. The accused men insisted that the government knew of their business transactions and had in fact sanctioned the commerce both for economic reasons and for the gathering of intelligence. Yet politicians signed public interest immunity certificates to prevent corroboration of their case going before the jury.

Not just one minister but four government ministers and the Attorney General were prepared to deny three men their defence to a criminal prosecution, which would most likely have led to their imprisonment. Liberty is one of the most precious rights we possess but here we had a case of politicians and civil servants preventing the truth from being told because it exposed the double standard of maintaining one thing in parliament and doing the opposite in private.

The malaise about ethics in public life often takes less dramatic forms, however, with the easy use of lies in public and no display of conscience when caught out; no sense of shame when politicians are found profiteering out of the policy on council house sales; a bullish refusal to resign when hypocrisy is exposed over sexual misbehaviour or when a contempt for the law has been displayed (by deporting a Zairian refugee in the face of a court injunction or changing the law on compensation for the victims of crime without going before Parliament) or when enormous sums of public money have been wasted (as in the Pergau Dam affair).

I have begun by expressing my concern that there has been a substantial erosion of values in public life because I believe it is important to look at these very public displays of immorality for a gauge of what is ailing Britain. We must ask ourselves how we can in our homes, schools and churches teach our children the development of conscience, the importance of truth, the concept of brotherly love, the need to take responsibility for our actions, without having those precepts contaminated daily by those who hold such sway over our lives.

And yet many of those people in public life would call themselves Christians. Defining a Christian, Ambrose Bierce said he was 'one who believes that the New Testament is a divinely inspired book suited to the spiritual needs of his neighbour'!

The last decade has seen individualism, consumption and blatant self-interest promoted into acceptable modes of behaviour. In this thrusting new world, the populace is divided into winners and losers, employed and unemployed, successful and unsuccessful and the measures of worth are those of 'value added' and 'cost effectiveness' and the ugly language of the market-place.

The nation was seduced by the notion that deregulation would let entrepreneurs run free in the money-markets making us all the beneficiaries of trickle-down economics. Instead, the divisions between rich and poor have become more marked. We have not seen everyone embraced by the benefits of such policies, but increasing exclusion which is posing a serious threat to social cohesion.

Aspects of British life, of which we rightly felt proud, are being undermined. There has been a denigration of public service so that those who chose to work in the fields of education, health care, social work, legal aid, the police, the probation or prison service are all seen as losers, lacking the entrepreneurial drive that is idealised in the present climate. Undervaluing of those crucial functions – the care of the sick or needy, the teaching of our young, the maintenance of the social fabric – engenders low morale, with the inevitable consequence that those activities become unworthy and, therefore, ineffective. In abandoning our economic destiny to the market-place we seem to be abandoning our moral destiny to it as well.

It is fashionable now to decry the 1960s as the decade when moral decay set in, when 'doing your own thing' was the motto of the day. Yet, for commitment to unrepentant individualism, the 1980s has perhaps greater claim to social destructiveness. This characterisation of decadent sixties' liberalism takes no account of the concern with moral imperatives such as war and peace, racial and sex discrimination, poverty and corruption – moral imperatives with which a generation became passionately engaged. There was no shame then in having a social conscience, no criticism of commitment to such issues as a manifestation of 'wetness' or the display of a bleeding heart. The sixties was the decade in which it was recognised that our society was no longer homogeneous and that anti-discrimination legislation was necessary in pursuit of equality and justice. Imposing one's views upon the unwilling was deprecated and a need for tolerance was identified as crucial to the well-being of the community.

In asserting the importance of individual conscience, however, insufficient regard was given to the responsibilities which flow from such intellectual self-sufficiency. Liberal theory laudably aims to maximise individual freedom but physical freedom divorced from all moral virtue does not secure long-term physical peace. We have undoubtedly seen a weakening of personal and familial responsibilities in recent years, but the Moral Majority response of seeking to invoke political authority and the law to enforce 'traditional values', with the emphasis being on sexual morality to the exclusion of anything else, is untenable in a modern pluralist democracy. The state's and the courts' legitimate concern, whether in moral or other matters, is and must be restricted to the public and social dimensions of human behaviour, to what concerns the community as a whole. But of course human activities are so interwoven that scarcely any are without some measure of social effect, and so most human behaviour affects the behaviour of others. It is the function of practical reason and judgment to determine to what degree and with what result individual activities affect public interests.

Members of an organised society need to share common goals and aspirations, what Lord Devlin our great jurist called 'the invisible bond which holds society together'. The last time there was any real discourse on the values which should inform the law was in the famous Hart–Devlin debate of the early sixties when, in response to the Wolfenden Report, Lord Devlin argued that society's shared morality was as necessary to its existence as a recognised government and the justification for its enforcement by law was simply that the law might be used to preserve anything essential to society's existence. (The Maccabean Lecture to the British Academy 1959 and thereafter in The Enforcement of Morals 1965.) Professor Hart countered with what was largely an invocation of John Stuart Mill that immorality should not be a crime and the test for the use of legal coercion should be whether the conduct harmed others (Law, Liberty and Morality 1962).

I do not want here to repeat the Hart–Devlin debate save in answering the central question, when considering Christian values, whether society still does have shared values and if so what those shared values are. Can we even talk about Christian values in the law when we live in a society of many races and religions and indeed in which the majority of people are not really religious at all. Like Hart I do not believe it is the law's role to enforce morals but I do believe that a set of principles and values should inform the law. Another great judge, Justice Frankfurter, who sat on the American Supreme Court, spoke of

Those agencies of mind and spirit which serve to gather up the traditions of a people, transmit them from generation to generation, and thereby create that continuity of a treasured common life that constitutes a civilisation (Minersville v Bobitis 310 US 586 1940).

The aspiration of freedom, which is itself a moral aspiration, is not enough to give direction to an organised society. Certain basic moral premises common to the Christian and Jewish traditions, in conjunction with the supporting religious premises, still constitute the fundamental moral horizons of most Americans and Europeans. To quote Habermas (*Postmetaphysical Thinking: Philosophical Essays,* 1992)

> We as Europeans cannot seriously understand concepts like morality and ethical life, person and individuality, or freedom and emancipation without appropriating the substance of the Judaeo-Christian understanding of history in terms of salvation.

Christian values are an inevitable and historic part of English law. Although over a century ago the view that 'Christianity is parcel of the laws of England' was disapproved by the courts (R v Ramsey and Foot 188315 Cox CC). We believe, for example, in monogamy as a moral principle and our law reflects it. It is there not because it is Christian but it certainly got there because it was Christian. The right of men to have more than one wife would be inimical now not just for religious reasons but because of women's expectations of equality. In Islamic societies the law usually reflects Islamic values. As Lord Devlin said, these acceptances are built into our house and could not be removed without bringing it down.

One of the last remaining areas where Christianity is overtly protected by the courts is in the law of Blasphemy. Before its dramatic resurrection by Mary Whitehouse in 1977 when she successfully prosecuted *Gay News* and its editor Denis Lemon, it had seemed that the offence of Blasphemy had died a natural death. In 1949 Lord Denning described the common law offence as a 'dead letter'. The offence is described in Stephen's 1950 *Digest of Criminal Law* as a publication which contains 'any contemptuous, reviling, scurrilous or ludicrous matter relating to God, Jesus Christ, or the Bible or the formularies of the Church of England as by the law established'. As you will appreciate, the unpleasant epithets about the Pope with which we were taunted as children in Glasgow or Northern Ireland would not be covered. This was very much an enactment to do with the Established Church.

In 1989 after the publication of Salman Rushdie's book, *The Satanic Verses*, and the issuing of a *fatwa* against him, a leading British Muslim applied for a summons alleging a blasphemous libel against the publishers on the grounds of insult to Allah and the prophet Mohammed. This was refused but leave was granted for Judicial Review. In a full and informative judgment, the court not only refused the application on the grounds that the law was clearly restricted to the Christian religion but went on to say:

We think it right to say that, were it open to us to extend the law to cover religions other than Christianity, we should refrain from doing so. Considerations of public policy are extremely difficult and complex. It would be virtually impossible by judicial decision to set sufficiently clear limits to the offence and other problems involved are formidable. These are considered at length in a Law Commission Report No. 145, Criminal Law Offences against Religion and Public Worship. We need only mention a few briefly. Among other matters, consideration would have to be given to the kinds of religions to be protected and to how religion is to be defined. [Would the Moonies be included

9

or the Church of Scientology?]. Although an English jury would be expected, or were in the last century expected, to understand the tenets of Christianity, this would not be so with other religions. There would be a need for expert evidence, no doubt, for both prosecution and defence. If different sects of the same religion had differing views and the published material scandalised one sect and not the other, how would the matter be decided? Since the only mental element is the intention to publish the words complained of, there would be a serious risk that the words might, unknown to the author, scandalise and outrage some sect or religion.

By implication this reasoning questioned the desirability of retaining the existing law.

At the same time the government through the then Home Office Minister sought to placate outraged Muslims in a long letter which included the passage 'an alteration in the law could lead to a rush of litigation which would damage relations between faiths. I hope you can appreciate how divisive and how damaging such litigation might be and how inappropriate our legal mechanisms are for dealing with matters of faith and individual belief. Indeed the Christian faith no longer relies upon it, preferring to recognise that the strength of their own belief is the best armour against mockers and blasphemers.'

For the same reasons the declared inclusion of Christian values into the law in contemporary society would in my view be divisive and excluding. Indeed, I believe that having an established Church is also an anachronism which should be abandoned. I thought it interesting that our King-in-waiting, when interviewed by Jonathan Dimbleby, not only admitted his own moral failings in the private sphere but displayed an unease at the role of King as Defender of the Faith, indicating that he saw the

Monarch more as a defender of Faith, specifically referring to the need nowadays to include the likes of Roman Catholics and Muslims. I think it is important for us as Catholics to remember that until as recently as 1974 no Roman Catholic could become Lord Chancellor and I remember when I first came to the Bar the gossip that Sir Peter Rawlinson, as he then was, might not be eligible because of his Catholicism. According to Lord Justice Balcombe's reading of *Halsbury's Statutes*, there are still doubts as to whether a Jew could be appointed to that office, which is ludicrous when so many of our finest and most principled judges among the Law Lords and elsewhere are Jewish, including the Lord Chief Justice.

In reality, of course, many of our values as Christians and as Catholics overlap with those of many non-Christians whether they be atheists, agnostics or people of other religions. (Bertrand Russell was once arrested for pacifist activity and on admission to prison was asked his religion and he said 'agnostic'. Whereupon the warder said, 'Agnostic, never heard of that one but I suppose you all believe in the same God'!)

We may not all believe in the same God, but could we not all believe in the same secular ethic? – an ethic which would be informed by Christian values but also profoundly valuable concepts from other traditions. Responsibility and respect for the elderly, for instance, seem to be far more entrenched in the Muslim tradition than in ours.

This may seem a very disappointing perspective to those of you who would like to think that the law should be drawing upon the catechism, with a clear set of Christian rules like the Commandments dictating human behaviour through the legal system. But I am afraid we have come a long way from the doctrine that 'error has no rights' and the days when the Magisterium, the Church's teaching authority, could set absolute parameters for morality with clear rules and fixed responses to breaches of them. Like it or not, Luther's assertions as to the role of the personal conscience challenged Europe's dominant moral philosophy and changed the course of history.

The Catholic Church has also felt its impact. While it is unlikely that we shall secure a conclusive resolution of this ongoing struggle between subjective and objective morality, we do have a duty, particularly as Christians, to ensure that a happier accommodation is found than that which currently exists. I believe that the law has to be religiously neutral but that by no means suggests that the law should be morally neutral. Indeed the English legal system invokes the test of the reasonable man in an effort to conjoin the subjective test for certain behaviour with objective standards.

In a democratic society, care should be taken so far as possible to avoid making laws which those subject to them find conscientiously objectionable, and to allow individuals and groups as far as possible, to decide how they shall live. But since moral decisions have to be made in the law, it is both right and the duty of Christians to enter into the public debate about those matters, like any other citizen, and seek to influence the outcome. Religion should not be privatised. Christians should not, though, have a prescriptive right denied to others to affect the outcome before any debate has taken place. If the Christian churches are to take their rightful place in the public forum of national life and contribute fruitfully in debates on issues of public policy and law they will have to do so on the basis of genuine respect for diversity. Churches are not the conscience of society or the state, though they may have important things to say to society and the state. They may by the same token have much to learn from other participants in public debates. An Irish theologian whom I greatly admire, Gabriel Daly OP, says churches sometimes convey the impression that they are wired for transmission only and not for reception. The case any church might wish to put must be argued in 'the marketplace of ideas', as Michael Perry says, 'in a manner neither sectarian nor authoritarian'. Fundamentalism of any creed is anathema to such an exchange of views and must be opposed by everyone who gives intellectual attention to their faith.

Vatican II's Declaration of Religious Freedom presupposes a readiness on the part of the Roman Catholic Church to argue its case in the democratic state but to acknowledge the rights of others. Debate means a process of rational argument. Those who will not listen exclude themselves from the debate.

I believe that Christ's teachings have much more to say about justice than about the law. My fellow Glaswegian, the writer William McIlvanney, says 'Who thinks the law has anything to do with justice? It is what we have because we can't have justice.' I was recently asked by a judge, who was concerned about society's demands for retribution in high profile cases, which produced great anger and desires for vengeance, what is justice? What does justice demand? I had just been engaged in some reading which had included St Thomas More – who should be every lawyer's patron saint – and the writings of some contemporary theologians, and with their lessons in mind struggled towards a rudimentary list of the components:

- justice involves the allocation of responsibility for offending and condemnation of it;
- it involves the assuagement of public outrage at the crime;
- it requires punishment;
- but another imperative of justice is an understanding of the wrongdoing, as well as compassion and mercy.

In all the demands for longer and tougher terms of imprisonment, the incarceration of yet more children, the return of the death penalty, Christ's message of forgiveness and redemption is lost.

Is Christ in the baying crowd which stones the prison van as it leaves the courthouse yard? Is Christ in the audience at party political conferences where the call is for yet more stringent regimes in the hells that are our prisons? Forgiveness and redemption are Christian values which should most certainly inform the law. Fairness, equality, non-discrimination are all Christian values.

In the 1991 national census a majority of the public expressed their loss of confidence in the criminal justice system. They perceived the courts as weighted in favour of the rich and privileged and believed that the system did discriminate, particularly against black people. Why are so many people now distrustful of an institution which formerly commanded their respect? Undoubtedly one factor is the change in public awareness. We have a more demanding and informed public which expects the professions, including the judiciary, to be accountable, which means taking responsibility. The same has already happened in medicine and education.

The perception that the courts are simply out of touch with the reality of people's lives poses a serious threat to justice. When the legal system fails, or is seen to fail, in the fulfilment of its practical function, society reaps the consequences. The law regulates our social relations. In doing so it issues messages which resonate throughout society and we internalise those communiques. The law therefore has a crucial role to play because democracy in itself does not always guarantee that we adhere to the highest principles.

Civilised men and women adhere to a social contract requiring them to settle disputes in courtrooms rather than with pistols at dawn. That involves the provision by the courts of symbolic retribution for the victims and their families as well as society, and the contract ceases to operate effectively if victims are not dealt with fairly in the courts or defendants cannot be guaranteed a fair trial. There is a constant tension between the needs of those who suffer crime and those who are accused of it and it is within that tension that justice is defined. There has to be a constant fine tuning to a changing world and a willingness to shed preconceptions. Real and generous shifts in attitudes and a restatement of our values are required to maintain confidence in the law.

Over the past few years we have witnessed a catalogue of miscarriages of justice: the Birmingham Six, the Guildford Four, the Maguires, the Tottenham Three, Stefan Kiszco, Jacqueline Fletcher, Judith Ward, and those who had been wrongly convicted at the hands of the West Midlands Crime Squad. One horror story has emerged after another about prisoners who had spent years maintaining innocence in the face of disbelief. It should be a source of pride to Catholics that Cardinal Hume was one of the people who spoke out about the concerns over the Guildford Four convictions.

The 'how' and 'why' that has racked the public conscience should have sent all judges and lawyers in search of an answer, a means of restoring faith in the concept of justice.

But I sometimes wonder whether the grand men of the law have really been chastened by the ghosts of trials past. In legal watering holes the miscarriages are too often dismissed as the regrettable mismanagement of criminal investigation by the police, while the campaigns for justice are slurred as the manipulation of procedural flaws by the politically motivated.

Cynicism, the enemy of justice, pervades the legal system. Christians should never be cynical. Far from being humbled by these recent experiences, there are still members of the judiciary who are resentful and angry that they have come under scrutiny at all. They claim that the system failed, not the personnel. All sorts of things are blamed to avoid the acceptance of responsibility: over-zealous policing or, at worst, police corruption in the face of crimes with a high emotional charge; inadequate protection for vulnerable defendants who had low intelligence or psychological problems and therefore made undetectably false confessions; scientists lacking in rigour and too closely connected to the police for independent professionalism. Judges and lawyers present themselves as innocent dupes, believing in the honesty and forbearance of the police and the experts.

This quote from Lord Denning, when he dismissed the attempt by the Birmingham Six to commence a civil action against the police, illustrates an attitude which permeated some of the judges' ranks during the Six's long and lonely campaign:

Just consider the course of events if this action is allowed to proceed to trial. If the six men fail it will mean much time and money will have been expended for no good purpose. If the six men win it will mean that the police are guilty of perjury, that they are guilty of violence and threats, that the confessions were invented and improperly admitted in evidence and the convictions were erroneous. That would mean that the Home Secretary would have to recommend they should be pardoned or remit the case to the Court of Appeal. This is such an appalling vista that every sensible person in the land would say it cannot be right that these actions should go any further. This case shows what a civilised country we are. The State has lavished large sums of money in their defence. On their own evidence they are guilty. It is high time it stopped because this is really an attempt to set aside their convictions. It is a scandal which should not be allowed to continue.

That view was not an aberration. It was shared by many less vocal colleagues. What happens to justice when the liberty of a citizen is less important than the reputation of the state?

The judiciary has, of course, been seen to respond: new methods have been sought and refined procedures advanced. The public is already being assured that many of the problems have largely been corrected by intervening legislative changes like the Police and Criminal Evidence Act 1984, which introduced tape-recorded interviews and additional checks on police procedure. A few more legal curlicues, some honing of the rules, a report here and there, mildly critical perhaps but not severe enough to undermine the status quo, and we can all get back to business.

But righting the wrongs within the legal system will require more than a review of methods. The injustices of the past come from something deeper than bad apple police officers or imperfect procedures. Again it is about rediscovering or reinventing the values which should underwrite the law.

The recent miscarriages of justice should remind us that it is only by keeping the legal tests for conviction very high that the courts can guarantee the protection of the innocent and maintain respect for the law. In virtually every one of the major miscarriage cases the backdrop was highly charged with emotion. In the cases of the Birmingham Six, Guildford Four and the Maguires, this was because of terrorist outrages; in the Tottenham Riot case it was because a policeman was hacked to death in a situation of racial tension; and in the Kiszco case it was because the sexually motivated murder involved a child. It was as though the burden of proof shifted to the defendants in these cases. Prove to us you are innocent was the unspoken demand and the protections which should be there for all of us were not. In almost all of these cases there were confessions by innocent people. The removal of the right to silence is a terrible assault upon the presumption of innocence and is an abandonment of one of our key legal principles.

I believe that just as society needs to hone a set of secular values and to reclaim our sense of the 'public good', so too do we need to establish a backdrop of principle within the law. It is my firm belief that a Human Rights discourse could help us greatly in achieving both.

It is important to remember that the roots of such a discourse are to be found in natural law. The founders of human rights law were arguably the Jesuits of Paraguay, who challenged the Conquistadores' treatment of the native Indians as defying the principles of natural law. The tenets of Human Rights Conventions sit very comfortably with a Christian perspective: respect for human life and the dignity and integrity of the individual; protection of the family, minorities, prisoners and the mentally ill; protection of religious and political freedom, right to a fair trial; equality.

To quote a book called *Human Rights and Responsibilities in Britain and Ireland – a Christian Perspective*:

Human Rights are a reflection of the justice which God requires in all human societies and the Christian can have no release from the constant endeavour to see justice upheld. There is indeed a strong and simple motive that impels Christians to demonstrate a profound concern for the poor, the weak and the oppressed. This is dominant in the Bible and continued throughout the Christian tradition. Christians believe that to pursue this tradition is to perform the will of God.

In *Pacem in terris*, Pope John XXIII gives supreme papal authority to that most secular of instruments, The Universal Declaration of Human Rights, reproducing virtually all its provisions. The Holy Father says a declaration of the rights and duties which the citizens and rulers should have towards each other ... should make it clear that the duties of the latter are to acknowledge, respect, harmonise, protect and promote the citizen's rights and duties ... In today's world the first thing to be looked for in a state's legal system is some sort of charter of fundamental human rights, expressed in clear and concise language and forming an integral element in the way a country is governed ... If any office holders violate or neglect to take account of human rights, they not only fail in their duty, they lose all authority to command obedience.

Well, here in Britain we still do not have a charter of human rights. We have not even incorporated the European Convention although we are signatories to it. Until people have a sense of themselves as citizens with rights and obligations to each other and to their community we will see fragmentation within our society. Whish is why I see constitutional change including a Bill of Rights as such a priority.

The comparative affluence of the late fifties and the sixties and the changes wrought in the post-war era had an enormous impact on the aspirations and expectations of British people.

The nature of society has altered considerably and social mores have adjusted. The role of women has changed. Our communities are no longer homogeneous but multi-racial, multi-cultural, multi-religious. We have come to expect more of everything rather than less. Patterns of employment have changed radically as a result of the technological revolution which seems to have taken place in the wink of an eye. There is hardly a household without phone and television and now even a computer. No office worth its name is not faxed, computerised and modemed up to the hilt. The key resource of the future will be knowledge – not capital, not natural resources, not even just labour, but knowledge. In the midst of such change there has been little reflection upon the ties which once bound us as a society and whether we know any longer what those ties are.

The implication of the technological revolution is enormous. There will be virtually no employment opportunities for those without the necessary knowledge and skills. The social consequences will be even greater and more insoluble than they ever were during the Industrial Revolution. When that revolution came, the homeless and unemployed teemed into the cities, sleeping in doorways, begging in the street, trailing problems with them which are all too familiar – crime, abandoned children, prostitution, back-street abortions and all the other wretchedness that goes with poverty. Police clamped down using newly introduced powers under the Vagrancy Acts not dissimilar to the new Criminal Justice Act – powers that became a weapon to protect those who had from those who had not. We may be seeing the beginning of similar social traumas. Any repeat now on the scale of the Industrial Revolution is a vista too frightening for words. It is something which no democratic country should be willing to countenance today. The way in which the law is harnessed in these new times will be crucial to the kind of society which develops. On the one hand there are pressures on the state to use the law coercively to contain state-produced problems and on the other there are campaigns for the law to become a more potent instrument for the protection of the citizen against the power of the state, as seen now in the increasing demand for a Bill of Rights.

Our vision of the future need not be a nightmare. We need not be hostages to a frightening tomorrow, in which we feel required to build walls to keep social decay out of sight. The challenge is enormous and will require a different set of priorities from those which currently engage our politicians.

It makes it all the more urgent that as a nation we should identify a shared value system and assert it in the public domain.

There can be no justice without social justice. Organised society should exist to enable members to perfect themselves both physically and morally. We would say in God's image and likeness. That means we have a duty to foster social conditions supportive of moral well-being. Justice is a good rallying cry for all of us. There is a beautiful poem by Juan Gonzales Rose:

> I ask myself now
> why I do not limit my love
> to the sudden roses
> to the tides of June
> the moons over the sea?
> Why have I had to love
> the rose and justice
> the sea and justice
> justice and the light?

I once heard Charles Handy speak about the creation of our wonderful cathedrals. Those magnificent edifices were built over hundreds of years, with master builders toiling over generations in their act of creation. Stonemasons raising their towering structures into the heavens, rarely seeing them in their finished state. Indeed at the outset of these great endeavours undertaken to the greater glory of God, the masons frequently had no idea whether the task was achievable – how, for example, the arch would be bridged to crown the final construction. But they believed that in the fullness of time engineering solutions would be found to complete their great projects. Theirs was an act of Faith.

I think we too must engage in an act of faith in the decisions we take now. We may not have all the answers in our quest for a better world but that should not prevent us from adopting a consistency of hope and faith. I believe our guiding principles should be justice, freedom and love.

Professor Michael Fogarty

President of the Movement for Christian Democracy
Vice-President of the Liberal Party

Michael Fogarty was educated at Ampleforth and at Christ Church, Oxford, where he gained his MA. Early in his career he was Official Fellow of Nuffield College, Oxford, and Professor of Industrial Relations, University of Wales, Cardiff. Later he was Director and Research Professor at the Economic and Social Research Institute in Dublin, and Senior Research Fellow and Deputy Director of the Policy Studies Institute (previously Political and Economic Planning and Centre for Studies in Social Policy).

Recently he has been involved in freelance policy and political research, particularly on business in the community and on recent developments in Christian Democracy in Western Europe, and is currently an Associate of Oxford University's Centre for European Politics, Economics and Society.

His publications include 'Christian Democracy in Western Europe', with recent follow-up articles; 'The Just Wage'; 'The Rules of Work'; 'Sex, Career and Family' and follow-ups. At various times he has been Chairman of the Catholic Social Guild, Chairman of the Newman Association, Vice-Principal of the Association of University Teachers, Vice-President of the Liberal Party, Chairman of Oxfordshire County Council and Chairman of several industrial relations enquiries in Ireland.

Professor Michael Fogarty
Christian Values in the Economy

The economy is about the creation of wealth through work. This chapter will show the breadth of what Christians understand by this, the reasons for the sense in which the Church has always stood for capitalism – in today's terms, for its 'Rhine' rather than its Anglo-American model – and how globalism now faces us with a Tower of Babel problem: how to redefine the globalised economy into 'manageable spaces'. It ends with a challenge to find the resources for autonomous think-tanks, to carry forward, from a Christian basis, the 'radical and long-term analysis' of the economy for which the Catholic Bishops' Conference called in its message for the General Election of 1987.

2

In the teaching of the churches, and in working documents such as the basic programmes of the Christian Democratic political parties, we have a distinctive Christian vision of a Responsible Society, including its economy. That vision, as the Pope reminded us in *Sollicitudo Rei Socialis*, is not an ideology in the sense of a blueprint to be imposed on the future or a prediction of what the future must inevitably be. What it offers is in the Pope's term 'orientations', guidelines to use in feeling our way forward in an uncertain world, and among these are guidelines on the purpose and operation of the economy. I divide what I have to say into three sections.

First, what do we expect from the economy? What do we look to it to deliver?

Second, how should the economy be organised to deliver what we expect of it? We live in a market, capitalist economy, and the market has been at the centre of discussion about the economy: so what, as Christians, do we make of it?

Third, it is one thing to have sound general principles, but another to know how to translate them into practical rules for managing a particular type of economy. Our economy has been through major changes in recent decades, and we in the Christian world have tended to be followers rather than trend-setters: late-comers who catch up with ideas instead of leading them, and who comment after the event on changes brought about by others under an agenda which they, not we, have set. Further major changes are on the way, and the same could easily happen again. What do we need to do if we are to become the trend-setters and to shape the agenda in our own way?

I What We Expect the Economy to Deliver

The creation of wealth
The purpose of the economy is the creation of wealth through work, and it is worth thinking about that definition for a moment. There is no problem about 'creation'. The world in which we live is shaped by those who work in the economy – entrepreneurs, technologists, artists, writers, office, factory, or service workers – all sharing in the most obvious way in God's work of shaping and redeeming creation. But 'wealth' is not so clear, for the 1980s produced a new heresy, the idea that there is a 'wealth-creating sector', taken usually to mean manufacturing and service businesses in the commercial market, on which all other activities in the economy are parasitic.

I think, for example, of the colleague who rose during a budget debate in the district council of which I was then a member to denounce the burdens which we were laying on that 'wealth-creating sector'. A surprising comment to make in that particular Conservative council, which was and is famous both for its low rates – Band D council tax for 1995/6 £1 – and for its skill in using public expenditure to promote private competitive enterprise. As our then leader used truly to say, to the discomfiture of opposition members like me (except that we too were rather proud of it), our council was the goose that laid the golden eggs. But let that pass, for I gave my colleague back a parable of a more personal kind.

Up the road from me, at that time, there lived Mr Mileson the supermarket owner, who from time to time supplied me with a bottle of wine wherewith to rejoice my heart.

Down the road lived Mr Gunning the heart surgeon, who supplied me, courtesy of the NHS, with a reconditioned heart wherewith to do the rejoicing. So, who was the wealth creator? By my colleague's test Mr Mileson was a true wealth creator, whereas Mr Gunning was a tax-fed parasite living off Mr Mileson's hard-won earnings. But I could show from my tax returns that even in the narrowest financial terms Mr Gunning's tax-fed services had been a splendid exercise in wealth creation. By putting me back in good earning condition he had increased the national income and the Inland Revenue's receipts by several times their cost, and incidentally had added the odd penny to Mr Mileson's turnover, to say nothing of the non-cash-measurable benefit to myself and my family, and perhaps even to the public from continuing my work as a councillor and chair of the local community association. And the fact that Mr Gunning was paid out of column 6 on my pay-slip, headed income tax, whereas Mr Mileson was paid out of column 7, net disposable income, was neither here nor there, for I had only one pay-slip and it all came out of the same pot. Mr Gunning, anyway, could easily have established his status in the 'wealth-creating sector' by moving a bit farther down the road and doing the identical job at the Thames Valley Nuffield Hospital with payment out of column 5: non-statutory contributions, for example BUPA.

The wealth which we as Christians look to the economy to provide is of every kind, cash-measurable or not. It includes capital in human resources as well as in buildings, machines, or roads, and returns from capital whether in dividends or in non-cash benefits, like the benefit to an owner-occupier of home ownership or to my village of its village hall. It includes flows of goods and services whether they are sold on the market or not, and benefits incidental to their production: employment, work satisfaction, good relations in the workplace, fairness in the distribution of rewards, whether achieved directly or through tax and social insurance, and stewardship of the physical environment. There might be less risk of misunderstanding if we talked, as certain German colleagues do, of the creation not of 'wealth' but of 'well-being for all'. And the workers from whom we expect these benefits may be in any sector: private or public, profit-making or non-profit, working in the informal economy of households, do-it-yourself, and voluntary caring networks, or for cash in hand in the grey to black market.

Operating rules

In delivering wealth and well-being, we expect people who work in the economy to follow certain guidelines: to operate, as in any other section of society, according to certain rules and to aim for certain objectives. Like every other field of human activity the economy has an ethic of its own. People working in it have their own specific calling from God, which they should be free to develop in their own way. That is the Calvinist concept of 'sphere sovereignty', which the Pope borrowed for the first time in *Centesimus Annus*. But the economy is also part of society, and in a Responsible Society there are common guidelines which apply in the economy as everywhere else.

The central point of reference is *the infinite and over-riding value of human personality*. We aim as Christians for a society which puts people first, setting out from the idea that women and men are made in the image of God and called by God to follow their destiny as individuals, as members of society, and as sharers and stewards in God's work of creation. The Pope has pointed out that the economy is a part of society where this is too easily forgotten. In *Laborem Exercens* he condemned the sin of 'economism', that is of driving economic theories beyond their useful limits, turning priorities upside down, and treating people as servants of economic processes instead of putting the economy at the service of people. He was thinking, of course, of the excesses of economic planning in the old Communist economies, but also of those of 'market economism' of the kind we have seen in recent years in the West.

From that central point of reference there follow five more specific aims which should be pursued in the economy as in the rest of society.

1 *Freedom and opportunity*, in the economy as elsewhere, as *Centesimus Annus* underlines; to take economic initiatives, to enjoy wider choice as economic performance improves, and, especially, to seek and find work, since 'the obligation to earn one's bread by the sweat of one's brow also presumes the right to do so'.

2 *Solidarity*, for one thing between the well-off and the deprived, the option for the poor; the economy must ensure fair shares in income and opportunity even for the poorest. But solidarity also has a more general meaning. A Responsible Society will be built round responsible and co-operative human relationships. It will be a community of communities from the family upwards, with each smaller community taking responsibility for its own destiny, but aware that it is also part of a larger whole and has a duty to work for the common good. So too the economy should be a community of communities based on partnership in enterprises and industries, on solidarity in trade unions, employers' organisations, and professional associations, and so on up to solidarity in the national and world economies.

3 *Stewardship*: sharing, that is, in God's work of creating and redeeming the world. In these green days we tend to think particularly of stewardship of the environment and of scarce world resources, but in *Centesimus*

Annus the Pope reminds us that stewardship of human resources is even more important, essentially because people come first, but incidentally because, as he says, human know-how is the economy's most important resource.

4 *Spread responsibility*, to use the Dutch term: the idea that the economy like the rest of society should be managed in a style consistent with the ideas of freedom and a community of communities. There should be strong leadership, in business as in government, but it should be enabling rather than authoritarian. Responsibilities should be spread in the way expressed in phrases like 'pluralism', 'social partnership', 'subsidiary function', or 'sphere sovereignty'.

5 *Evolution*, A Responsible Society will change and progress, but be suspicious of grand blueprints for the future. It will face conflicts and work through them when they come, recognising that hard bargaining can be needed. The Church has never, for example, denied the right to strike. A Responsible Society will look for progress first and foremost, not through class war, confrontation, and violence, but through the diffusion of ideas and peaceful negotiation. *Centesimus Annus* reminds us how the apparently impregnable structure of Communism in Eastern Europe collapsed, not through violent revolt, but peacefully through change in the minds and hearts of the people.

II   Christians and the Role of the Market

Managing the economy: the role of the commercial market
If the purposes of the economy and the rules by which it should work are as wide-ranging as I have suggested, then

managing the economy has so many angles that I cannot hope to cover them all. I am going to focus instead on one aspect of the economy which in recent years has been central. Where do we in the Christian world stand on the question of the competitive commercial market?

The simple and flat answer is that the Church stands and always has stood for capitalism, the competitive market economy, and so do, and always have done, Christian-inspired political movements like the Christian Democrats: but not, of course, for any kind of capitalism. Writers like Michel Albert distinguish between the Anglo-American model of capitalism which has many of the marks of 'market economism', and the other capitalism, sometimes known as the Rhine model, shaped in Western Europe largely under Christian Democratic influence, and paralleled without benefit of clergy (or anyway of our clergy) in Japan. It is for that 'other capitalism' that we as Christians stand.

I could show what the Church has meant by the 'other capitalism' from encyclicals – read for example what *Centesimus Annus* has to say about local and globalised markets, competition, and the role of business people – or from bishops' pastorals, like the American bishops' 1986 pastoral on *Economic Justice for All*, or by taking the story right back to the scholastic writers of the Middle Ages, as I did in my book on *The Just Wage*. But I myself learn better from practice, and I take as a particularly good source the chief architect of the 'other capitalism' in its modern form, Ludwig Erhard. As head of the economic administration of West Germany just after the Second World War he fathered the idea of the social market economy, and in so doing brought about the German 'economic miracle' and wrote a new chapter in Christian thinking about the economy. His story is particularly interesting because, though his personal background was Evangelical, he was not from the Christian stable in the sense of working from traditional Christian social teaching. His ideas grew out of his experience as a professional economist and market researcher, and, exactly as Newman used to predict, the honest pursuit of secular understanding led him right into the Christian tradition.

Erhard was much more than a technical economist. He had a vision of 'well-being for all', certainly with rising incomes and full employment, but above all in and through what he called a 'formed' society. By that he meant a society characterised by personal and shared responsibility, solidarity, and the overcoming of class differences, thanks not only to economic progress but to the opening of minds through knowledge, education, participation, 'true leisure', and the arts: exactly our Christian vision of the Responsible Society. And on the role of competitive markets in such a society he had two things to say.

First, a properly competitive market matches up to the standards which I have just outlined. It is the order which guarantees the direction of production towards the real needs of consumers and towards meeting overall needs at the lowest cost and with the smallest input of political and social power. It opens the way to freedom and opportunity through scope for individual and collective initiative and through rising incomes and wider choice. It spreads responsibility and bars the way to concentrations of economic power, whether in the hands of private owners or of the state. It is *the* mechanism for evolutionary change. And, while market competition rests on freedom of initiative and choice, it is not a formula for mere individualism. A well-functioning market not only leaves room for solidarity but, as will appear in a moment, positively requires it.

But, second, a market can be relied on to produce results like these only if it is as Erhard used to say 'planfully influenced' and operates within an externally determined framework, for Adam Smith's 'hidden hand of the market' is self-regulating only up to a point. Markets need parameters of three kinds: public regulation, people with the right qualities and resources, and partnership in the 'middle field' between the state and the individual. And what is distinctive about the Christian approach is the emphasis which it lays on the second and third of these, and especially on the third.

Public regulation

I do not mean that we Christians play down the role of governments, central banks and international agencies such as the European Union or World Trade Organisation in regulating the economy, Far from it; we have in the concept of 'public justice' as developed in Christian thinking in recent years a high and positive ideal of the role of government in the economy as elsewhere, and a long agenda, for many of the parameters of markets are of a kind which only governments or governmental-type agencies can provide or guarantee. Markets need law, including laws to protect market competition itself, and law enforcement. They need infrastructure, physical and in areas like education, training, and science and technology. They need a framework of geo-graphical/environmental planning to keep local and regional development in balance and to protect the environment. The buzzword for Christians today is no longer the 'social' market but the 'eco-social' or 'ecological and social' market.

Markets need a stable currency, so long as that is understood as a convenience and not as a straitjacket, for there must also be, as Erhard used to point out, and some of his successors may have forgotten, fiscal, financial, and public investment policies to prevent deflationary crises and mass unemployment and oil the wheels of change. Some of us older people remember how comparatively little protest there used to be when the work force in industries like mining and the railways was run down literally by the hundred thousand in the 1950s and 1960s, because in those days of Erhardian or Keynesian macro-economics there was always, somewhere, another job to go to.

Last but not least, only governments can guarantee a safety net for those whom market forces leave behind. Christian thinking about the economy has never been egalitarian, in the sense of aiming at equal outcomes and bringing everyone to the same level. If we call, as we do, for economic freedom and opportunity, then we have to accept that people will use their opportunities in different ways and with differing success. But, since we also call for solidarity, there has in the end to be a guarantee, and in the last resort a public guarantee, of a reasonable minimum for all.

But, though our agenda for governments' contribution to the framework of markets is long and heavy, it is still limited by the ideas of subsidiarity and of society as a community of communities. It includes only items which cannot be provided for at lower levels or by more 'communitarian' means. In devising parameters for markets we as Christians think from the bottom up, and so, first of all, about the contribution to expect from developing the qualities and resources of the people.

People

Adam Smith insisted that we owe our dinner not to the benevolence of the butcher and baker but to their self-interest, courtesy of the hidden hand of the market, but neither he nor the other founding fathers of modern market economics ever suggested that selfishness was enough. They took it as read that markets work better if their participants have integrity, responsibility, and ethical and religious motivation. So before them did the mediaeval scholastics. Henry of Langenstein, back in the fourteenth century, gave the argument a special twist by showing that unethical conduct not only corrupts the market in detail –

cowboy bricklayers and carpenters, for him, were 'impious workers destined for hell' – but is at the root of inflation; for a community whose citizens are 'abstemious and virtuous' will enjoy a lower and steadier cost of living than one full of people who are 'greedy, voluptuous, avaricious, and grasping'.

In the Christian tradition we have never denied that a well-organised market can bribe or bully even people who are 'greedy, avaricious, and grasping' into giving customers what they want. But we insist that markets will run to better purpose, and with less friction, if they are lubricated with justice, love, and compelling faith. People in markets need an ethical code, courtesy perhaps of the Institute of Business Ethics. They need to appreciate the meaning of solidarity and of membership in a community, for their decisions affect others, and they have a duty to take these others' interests as seriously as their own: which is, of course, the definition of loving one's neighbour as oneself. And, as Bishop Lehmann, the chairman of the German Bishops' Conference, reminded the German Christian Democrats a couple of years ago when they were redrafting their *Programme of Principles*, even codes designed by Christians may be sounding brass and tinkling cymbals unless those who apply them are inspired by 'the strength of living faith'.

If people are to contribute as much as they might to the economy and the market, however, they need more than just the right principles. They also need resources with which to act, and this has been a constant theme in Christian social teaching. Traditionally, the emphasis has been on enabling people to acquire property, real property in the home, the farm, or the small business, or cash savings or shares. But resources mean more than simply property in that traditional sense. To contribute effectively, or even to survive, in a changing and technically advancing modern economy people need, as *Centesimus Annus* says, 'know-how', up-to-date knowledge and experience developed through lifetime learning. And, above all, they need to have acquired 'capacity to cope', the capacity to change, adapt, and reach out for or create new opportunities. 'Capacity to cope' is important in every field. I learnt a lot about it from looking through the files of the Catholic Marriage Advisory Council for factors in the survival or breakdown of marriages, and again from studies of success or otherwise in the transition to retirement. And, of course, in today's flexible and ever-changing economy, where the idea of a lifetime career with a single employer or in a single range of skills is becoming a thing of the past, 'capacity to cope' is essential both for personal and family survival and for flexibility and dynamism in the working of the economy.

Partnership
Finally, as their third parameter, markets need partnership. That has been the Church's tradition since far back in the Middle Ages, and in modern times the ideas of partnership in the enterprise and industry, of collective agreement, consensus, and self-regulation by the 'social partners', run right through the encyclicals from *Rerum Novarum* onwards. They follow naturally, of course, from the ideas of solidarity and of a community of communities. But when it comes to application in practice, this is an area where we as Christians have a problem on our hands. For whereas Christian ideas about partnership have had and still have a major impact in the countries of the 'other capitalism', they have in recent years become much less acceptable in those of Anglo-American capitalism.

Let me take a couple of illustrations from the 'other capitalist' countries. Historians of the origins of the social market sometimes give the impression that *Mitbestimmung*, the German version of employee involvement through trade unions, statutory works committees and co-determination, against a background of industry-wide collective bargaining, was an optional extra to keep the trade unions and the British Labour government happy. Far from it. For Konrad Adenauer the point was 'social responsibility rather than socialism'. If the labour market needed regulation, then better self-regulation than over-reliance on regulation by the state. Ludwig Erhard saw educating people in the realities of the market and the economy as essential to his vision of a social market in a 'formed' society. A particularly good way to do it – and incidentally to provide a safeguard against abuse of the kind common under German capitalism in earlier years – was to involve them in key decisions directly, responsibly, and with full access to information.

Thirty years on, you find Dutch Christian Democrats drafting their basic programme, *Points of Departure*, and arguing on similar lines. In an up-to-date, competitive and socially responsible economy money has to be found out of the product of enterprise for many purposes running beyond what market pressures and enterprises' immediate, short-term interests can be relied on to enforce: long-term investment and job creation, for example, rather than instant profit, or lifetime learning for the whole work force rather than a patchwork of ad hoc training, or systematic action to incorporate disabled workers and other disfavoured groups. And that money has to be found without either skimping on the Just Wage or raising costs and prices beyond competitive levels, putting firms out of business, and creating a spiral of inflation.

So, whose business is it to do these things? The Dutch Christian Democrats' answer, in line with their and our understanding of 'spread responsibility' and of the economy as a community of communities, is that this responsibility lies in the first place with the community of those working in each enterprise or industry. They may not like it, for, as the Dutch very bluntly put it, the result will necessarily be that less of the proceeds of enterprise is available to distribute in pay and dividends than people might wish. They may not be very good at it, and, in accordance with the rule of subsidiarity, the state may have to step in from time to time to correct or supplement what the 'social partners' do. But 'we must get away from state-market thinking', the idea that the only alternative to unrestrained market forces is regulation by the state, which is in any case overloaded. And, following Erhard's line of thought, there is merit in confronting people as directly as possible with the reality and costs of necessary decisions, and not allowing them to dodge issues by leaving them to the politicians.

If you have followed recent discussion of the Social Chapter of the Maastricht Treaty, you will have noticed an assumption that any improvement in employees' conditions such as that Chapter proposes means a net addition to the costs of employment, which will damage competitiveness and prospects for employment. But that, on our Christian understanding, is to miss the point completely. The real question is not about *adding* to costs but about *sharing* what can be earned in a properly competitive market, and it is precisely on that question of sharing that the partnership approach to decision-making focuses attention.

Finally, if you ask in a more general way why the partnership approach kept so much appeal in the countries of the 'other capitalism', one simple answer is that for years, on the most hard-headed economic calculation, the Rhine model in either its German 'social market' version or its more corporatist Alpine version, in Switzerland and Austria, regularly out-performed Anglo-American capitalism.

And yet the Christian tradition of partnership has lost some of its appeal, even in the 'other capitalist' countries, and still more so in the world of Anglo-American capitalism.

Here in Britain a consensus and partnership economy developed in the first decades after the Second World War.

It matched in many ways the ideas of the churches and had considerable approval from them: but it is gone. Since the 1970s, trade unionism and collective bargaining have taken a beating, and the defence of them not long ago by the Catholic Bishops' Conference fell flat as a pancake. British employers score low on a Europe-wide comparison of the use made of unions and works councils to raise major issues with their staff. Our government secured for large British firms operating in Europe a formal opt-out from the Maastricht provisions for Europe-wide joint consultation; though the opt-out is only formal, since more firms from Britain than from any other country have been caught by these provisions, precisely because so many also operate elsewhere in Europe where the opt-out does not apply.

The idea of teamwork in the works community looks passé in an economy where the captain of the team expects to collect not only the cup but the lion's share of the cash, while his or her downsized and de-layered team-mates pick up pay cuts and P45s. We seem to be hearing more about the company as the business of the shareholders and less, till very recently, about the enterprise at the service of all its stakeholders. Self-regulation has been tried and too often found wanting. And if in Britain today you want to risk whispering, very quietly, a really politically incorrect word, try 'corporatism'.

The pendulum may well swing back. The climate is changing, the neo-conservative ideas of the 1980s are fading into history, and new, more 'communitarian' ideas are on the way. The new directions of the 1980s, in other countries as well as in Britain – Switzerland and Austria, for example, since I have just mentioned them – were the work of women and men in a hurry, and with a touch of tunnel vision: people who heard voices telling them just what to do, and to do it fast. There is a message well known to experimental social scientists as well as to Japanese managers and Swiss politicians. If you know exactly what is to be done, then by all means act now and waste no time on consultation. But you had better be genuinely sure that you do know it, because, if you are feeling your way into a not-so-certain future, and need to be sure you are asking the right questions before jumping to the answers – and if anyway you need to carry the people along with you – then it is wiser to take the road of consultation and partnership, for the long way round may well prove to be the shortest way home.

But, though the years of tunnel vision are passing, there is still a battle to be fought by those of us who stand for the Christian tradition of partnership; and that will require us too to rethink, for not all the 1980s criticisms of 'corporatism' were unjustified. Too often Christian thinkers, politicians, and business people were left behind, at a loss, with their intellectual knickers in a twist, while others raced ahead. And that brings me to my main message.

III Shaping and Delivering the Message

Do we know how to manage the market?
Let us face it squarely. We know the principles on which markets should be managed. But do we – and in this case I mean not only Christians but any of our economic or political leaders – know just how to do it in practice? I owe a useful analogy here to a colleague, Jonathan Thomas, in the Association of Christian Economists. It is that of the Tower of Babel.

You remember the story of Babel. The peoples of the earth got above themselves and started to build a mighty city reaching to heaven. The Lord looked down and said 'These people are presumptuous: they are promoting themselves beyond the limit of their ability, I will show them,' and he set them chattering to each other at incomprehensible cross-purposes, so that they had to give up their grand project and do something more sensible, like building cities of manageable size. I wonder, as my colleague mused in a paper last year, whether on the question of the management of the economy we are not back to Babel now?

We were there before, of course. I remember very well from my time as an economics student the confusion of voices and policies on economic issues which prevailed into the 1930s. In Britain as in other countries, with the help of great practical thinkers like Keynes and Erhard, we did then learn how to manage our national economies, and the prosperity of the post-war years resulted. Now, however, we have built vast new economic spaces: the European Union with its fifteen countries and more to follow, and the globalised economy. Do we know how to manage economies on this vastly increased scale, in the style for which our Christian vision leads us to hope, according to the rules and for the purposes which I have set out? Are we in control? Looking round the world as it is, from unemployment in Europe to poverty, debt, and environmental disaster in the Third World, and not forgetting the results of playing Masters of the Universe on computers in Singapore, it does not look as if we are. Never mind Babel; my own analogy is of a bunch of teenagers who break into a BMW and drive off into the dusk at a hundred miles an hour, hoping that all will be well.

Perhaps we shall learn once again, but that will certainly mean thinking thoughts that have not been thought of so far, and in current terms might be unthinkable. When the German Christian Democrats were revising their *Programme of Principles* they brought together a conference of experts to discuss the draft. Among those invited for the section on the family was a television producer, Petra Gerster, famous for a series called *Mona Lisa*, after the lady with the enigmatic smile: and she gave them the enigmatic smile with a vengeance. You have, she said, impressive proposals for promoting the stability and security of families, and others for promoting the country's competitive position in the new globalised economy. But have you not noticed that your two sets of proposals are at cross-purposes? If we mean business about the family, do we really want 'an economic system whose ideal worker is a celibate without commitments or family responsibilities, committing all his energy to the business, and ready to be shoved around by it in the world at will'? – a system which can function only on the basis of ignoring children and old people, and where values are determined by the market instead of governing it? As to what should be done, some of Ms Gerster's proposals were fairly mild, like keeping Sunday special, but then she really went to town. Should we not, she said, take a leaf out of the book of the French? They have a certain style of living and are determined to preserve it. Should we not do the same, if necessary behind the walls of a Fortress Europe, 'even if all the market economists scream like a horde of devils sprinkled with holy water'?

Well, how politically incorrect can you get? Trust a television person to hype an issue to make a point. There are of course two sides to this as to other questions. *Centesimus Annus* reminds us that there is actually a lot to be said for globalisation of the economy, and some developing as well as economically advanced countries have done rather well out of it. Nevertheless, there is a lot of work still to be done if we are to find how to reconcile the undoubted advantages of open markets, Euro or global, with stability and security for people, families, and local communities. We need to think again, like the builder of Babel, about how to create manageable spaces fit for people to live in, while still benefiting from the opportunity and flexibility of the vastly enlarged open market. And we need to do our thinking both at the macro-level, as in the current debate over the future of the European Union, and at the more detailed level being explored by, for example, the 'Demos' group. The title of a paper read by Professor Ian Taylor at the Tavistock Institute last week asks the key question: *Is There an Alternative to a Global Market Society?*

Delivering and developing the message

When we have developed our Christian message about the economy further, we shall of course have to see that it is effectively delivered. Let me begin by putting that point about delivery out of the way: for in this country we in the Christian world have not been too successful in delivering even the message which we already have.

The Church of England, for example, has never got across to the public the riches of its own social and economic thinking. When I say 'riches', I mean it. From 1971 to 1991 the Board for Social Responsibility alone produced 236 reports and papers bearing on our vision of the Responsible Society.

There is plenty of very good thinking there, as I bear personal witness, since for some years I was a Catholic co-optee on the BSR. But how many people here can lay their hands on their hearts and say that they understand what all this thinking by the C of E amounts to? The C of E does not of course have a Pope to pull it all together and put the stamp of authority on the result. But for the purpose I have in mind it does not need a Pope. What it could do with is a William Beveridge. I worked at one time alongside one of the teams getting together the material for what became the Beveridge Report. Here was a vast and confusing variety of views flowing in from all quarters, yet with lines of consensus running through it. Beveridge did not invent that consensus, but he succeeded brilliantly, like the first-class civil servant that he was, in pulling it together and giving it shape.

In the Catholic Church we do have a Pope who pulls it all together, yet we still have something of the same problem. At one time I made a collection of statements by our own bishops on economic and other policy in the Thatcher years, based on the Church's official documents and bishops' own observation of what they saw happening to their people on the ground. That collection added up to a powerful critique of the 'market economism' of those years, but, as in the case of the C of E, the message was delivered piecemeal. It was not pulled together or brought into the focus needed for maximum impact on the Church and the public.

What really struck me about those statements, however, was something different, not about delivery but about the message itself. Our bishops' comments always come late, after the event, and not at the decisive stage when ideas and policies take shape. If we are to be trend-setters in economic and social thinking we have to develop the message in good time, and that means starting very early, for the roots of major changes in the social and economic agenda lie very far back. Lord Harris, the founder of the Institute of Economic Affairs, one of the think-tanks whose work led to the neo-conservative revolution of the 1980s, once told me that he began to 'think the unthinkable' away back in the totally different climate of the 1950s. It took twenty years of hard and systematic work by his and other groups to get the 'unthinkable' seriously thought about, and thirty to see it translated into government policy and legislation. Friedrich Hayek, the grandfather of recent market economism, wrote his first contribution to 'thinking the unthinkable' far enough back to be on my reading list as an undergraduate in the 1930s.

That is the sort of time-scale on which we have to think if we are to be trend-setters shaping the future of society, not merely followers bringing up the rear. In their message for the General Election of 1987 our bishops stressed the need for 'radical and long-term analysis', in the light of our Christian principles, of the problems of employment and the economy which happened to be the central issues in that election; but they had also to point out that this analysis had not been done, and so had to leave judgment on them aside. I am afraid that that could happen again. True the climate is changing in a direction more favourable to the Christian tradition. But we still need to be thinking now about what may perhaps be, or be made to be, the agenda for 2020 or 2050.

Moreover, for thinking that far ahead we need our own specialised long-range think-tanks; and they had better not be too official, for long-range 'thinking of the unthinkable' is necessarily speculative, a form of licensed lunacy which does not fit well into official machinery. We learnt a lesson about that in the days after Vatican II when the Catholic Bishops' Conference was founded, and in turn established a set of Commissions. These Commissions, Justice and Peace and so on, were autonomous and free-floating. I do not think that anyone accused them of heresy or even of going very far in 'thinking the unthinkable', but, as they pushed ahead into fresh thinking and published their ideas, they flooded the bishops with more material than they could digest, yet, because they were official agencies of the CBS, appeared in their publications to give their ideas at least an informal stamp of episcopal authority. Quite rightly, the bishops reined them in and made their secretariat what it is today, a civil service working within the limits of what the bishops immediately need and can themselves handle.

For 'radical and long-term analysis' on a Christian basis we need autonomous think-tanks with a continuous corporate existence and, looking round the churches, I do not see anything which quite fills the bill. I do not underestimate the activity of, for instance, the Institute of Business Ethics or the Association of Christian Economists:

still less that of Edinburgh University's Centre for Theology and Public Issues or the new Centre for Faith and Culture at Westminster College, Oxford. But I wonder if even the two latter are not too official for what I have in mind. A fully equipped think-tank is expensive. With a substantial in-house team, like that of my former employer the Policy Studies Institute, you head rapidly for a seven-figure budget: though you can also, like IEA, cut the cost by out-sourcing. But, one way or another, think-tanks undertaking 'radical and long-term analysis' we must have.

I end with a simple thought. Is there anyone who would like to put down the cash, individually or by way of a consortium, to back a think-tank full of lunatic but professionally expert Christians of whatever denomination, 'thinking the unthinkable' and conducting 'radical and long-term analysis' of the economy as it may develop or be made to develop over the next thirty to sixty years?

Hugo Young

Author and Journalist

Hugo Young was born in 1938, educated at Ampleforth College and read law at Balliol College, Oxford. After starting in journalism on the *Yorkshire Post*, he spent eighteen years on the *Sunday Times*, where he became Political Editor and later Deputy Editor.

He has won several British Press Awards for his political writing and now writes a political column twice weekly in the *Guardian*. He has been named as Columnist of the Year in the British Press Awards for 1980, 1983 and 1985. He has jointly published several books and his biography of Margaret Thatcher, *One of Us*, was warmly received.

Hugo Young
Christian Values in the Media

The modern media pay lip-service to Christian values, but have long since ceased to promote them. Future trends in television and the press seem set to increase hostilities. Who is to blame – or are media values and Christian values irreconcilable?

3

Christian Values and the media are different from the subjects of other chapters of this book. I feel I've drawn the short straw. The fact that this is the territory where Rupert Murdoch, the most powerful man in the world, is widely confused with God should not deceive anybody into believing there is common ground between us. Mapping a path towards reconciliation, and even shared celebration, is a task that makes the cleaning of the Augean Stables seem elementary, and I should warn you that I am not going to attempt it.

I should state my limited credentials for this chapter: I come as a journalist and a Christian, but not, I have to say, a notably Christian journalist. If I write from a Christian position, it is quite deeply concealed. I like to think I try to live by at least some of the Christian values, but I recoil from any sense of mission. Perhaps I can see in myself, therefore, part of the problem I'm approaching. Catholic faith is one thing, the practice of journalism something not hostile to it but rather detached from it. Like a lot of journalists I'm a professional outsider. This is an incorrigible habit, my way of looking at the world. The values are there, but as a kind of background hum. In political journalism, which is where I work most, I abhor allegiance. So my stance is as a journalist looking mainly at the media and partly the Church, and not as a Christian journalist looking at Christianity.

And then I've got a more important disclaimer to make. The media cover a vast field of performance, and I must decide what I am qualified to talk about. All aspects of public communications give rise to questions of interest to public moralists, which is one thing Christian teachers offer themselves as being. I think it will be helpful from the start to make clear, in an ecumenical spirit, that I prefer to stake no unique claim for Christian values, but rather see myself as talking about values that are shared by many religions: that is, the broad values of charity and community, decency and hope, integrity and truth, which are promoted far beyond the narrowing pale of the Christian Churches. I shall have nothing to say about advertising, for example, nor about films and theatre and even books. I shan't primarily be concentrating on entertainment either, though of course that comes into any discussion of television. Also, I don't want to get drawn into the specific field of how religion is reported, or what priority it is given in the media.

No, my main interest is in how these values, those of the media and the Churches, play off against each other in that area of what I like to call aspirational truth-telling. The most important function of the media, I argue, is trying to make sense of the real world: not necessarily to discover The Truth, a task certainly best left to priests and presbyters, but to give the telling of near-truth their best shot. How in this world – of news and documentaries on television, of so-called reality as it is presented in the press – do the media succeed in factoring in recognisably Christian values? And, to ask a sharper question, what is the Church's role, its own special contribution to the task which I define as the most important one, where *its* values, as well as the media's, are put to the test?

There is more to be said about the media here than about the Church, so I will start with the Church. The implication behind the title of this chapter – indeed, all of them – is that it is the values of the *worldly* world, in this case the media world, that stand in constant need of testing by reference to the Christian. It is the newspapers and television that do not measure up to some higher ideal that Christianity and its prophets, both ancient and modern, lay down. These days, the Churches tend to disguise this claim behind veils of humility, presenting themselves as puzzled supplicants at Murdoch's temple. In one of his big speeches on the subject, Cardinal Martini, Archbishop of Milan, complained in 1990 that 'we have no mediatic consciousness' [I quote from an exotic translation]. 'We are awkward in communication', he went on. 'We have an inferiority complex before the great secular press or television or radio. We still don't know or appreciate the new language of the media with the insistence on connotation and vibration.' And it is true enough that the Vatican does not easily resonate on its only rival for global reach, the CNN television network. It has found no equal way of counteracting what the Cardinal called 'the world of violence, pornography and a shallow vision of life'.

All the same, we should be clear that the values expressed and acted on by the Church are not always congruent with the kind of media that are of the greatest social importance. There is a clear disjunction between Christian values, at least as expressed by the Roman Church, and those of good journalism. This is decidedly not an area where we can say with confidence that if only Christian qualities were more in evidence, the media would be doing a better job.

In recent years, the Vatican has gone through different phases in its declarations about what the media should aspire to be. The Pastoral Instruction of 1971, on the application of Vatican II to social communication, had an other-worldly quality, far removed from the universe of the *Sun* or even the *Guardian*. Gazing with admiration upon the technical possibilities even then available, it purred hopefully about how these might be used 'to build new relationships', helping people 'to know themselves better and to understand one another more easily'. It saw the new media as inclining people 'to justice and peace, to goodwill and active charity, to mutual help'. It proposed a new mission statement for the *News of the World*: 'the cultivation of that charity among men which is at once the cause and the expression of fellowship'.

What this emphasises is the gulf of purpose between the media and the Churches, which is simply a fact of life and not a discreditable one to either side. The Church, in all its teachings, stresses the value of doing good. When discussing the difference between good and bad films, the same Vatican document of 1971 saw one of the definitions of a good film as being one that 'would contribute to moral progress'. In its own missionary work, the Church can never be a mere observer. It sees in all God's creatures, including editors and journalists, a capacity for achieving or not achieving the kind of social good in which it is interested, which does not, on the whole, include the kind of value-free search for a secular truth which a lot of the best journalism is about. I shall come later to the moral consequences of the modern media, but it should be said straightaway that 'doing good' is seldom the stated purpose of even the most hypocritical among them. The Pastoral Instruction was full of this kind of utopian guidance, delivered, however, in an unimposing tone of voice, which contained a fair amount of understanding as to why Utopia might never come to pass.

With its successor document, *Aetatis Novae*, in 1992, a harsher tone is evident. We sense a new régime of firm instruction, where the task of the media is defined more explicitly as being to proclaim the gospel – and where the more secular functions are given shorter shrift. And this, I suggest, offers a more accurate reflection of a divide between Church and media in which Christian values, thus expressed, are unhelpful to good journalism. For the Church has always had a rather exclusive connection with the search for truth. In its long history, the Vatican has been an agent of censorship and propaganda – more or less stringent, as the centuries came and went – which set it in an entirely different tradition from the free press.

Some aspects of religious truth-telling are, of course, untouchable. There is a sense in which religious truth is for ever alien to the deconstructive procedures of modern journalism. Religious truth is about otherness, about mystery, about the impalpable. It makes a claim to permanence, in a media environment dominated by transience. It addresses the deepest roots of myth and faith. Such truths present a challenge to secular inquiry which it invariably trivialises, and can never meet without descending into hopeless vulgarity and ending in embarrassing failure. The Church must be defended in its claim that some things are sacred. God and his interpreters are not properly susceptible to the reductivist simplicities of the *Daily Mail*.

But in its disciplinary mode, the branch of the Church run from the Vatican is in some ways the enemy of truth-seeking. Nobody seems to take the Index seriously these days, but the prohibition of books was one announcement of the Roman attitude to free enquiry ranging far beyond matters theological. And the mentality of prohibition lives on. Not long ago, I attended mass at Brompton Oratory – it was during the debates about *Veritatis Splendor* – and heard from the pulpit a characterisation of those debates as, and I quote, 'the voice of Satan'. Only Satan, it seemed, could be asking the Pope a critical question. I could not decide which was the more remarkable: the beardless youth of the priest who confidently sent forth this utterance, or the unstartled acquiescence of the ageing congregation that was present in the Oratory that Sunday.

The Oratory may be a slightly aberrant case. But the same kind of mentality – authoritarian, defensive, anti-truth – is, for example, still frequently to be observed in the Irish Church, by far the strongest religious institution in these islands. No one can be entirely unsympathetic to the travails of churchmen caught in situations of sexual compromise, and even to those of the authorities who have to cope with the consequences. But the cover-ups and denials attending the exposure of the Bishop of Galway in 1992, and the similar performance last year over the paedophile priest who was an accessory before the fact of the fall of Albert Reynolds's government, reminded the world of the Catholic Church's powerful tendency, in some countries, to consider its interests to be above and beyond those of society at large, and not properly amenable, if it can possibly be avoided, to the normal procedures of truth-telling which should be the media's highest purpose.

The Catholic Church, in short, presents a problem for even the responsible element of the communications industry. It is not entirely happy to play its part in the process of free and honest inquiry. No longer – if it ever was – able to exert authority over a deferential media-world, it seems now frightened of it and often responds by retreating from it, sometimes by misleading it. At bottom, it does not believe in the same journalistic rules as the secular world. The life, therefore, of the editor of a Catholic paper is particularly tricky. And in that regard I should like to pay an admiring tribute to the editor of *The Tablet*, John Wilkins, who navigates so brilliantly between the expectations of his readers and the impositions of his Church – and has doubled the paper's circulation in the process.

What, however, is ranged *against* the upholder of Christianity? Having tried to show that, in my part of the media, the violation of values is not all one way, what is there to be said about the media generally? The Church, I argue, is no friend of secular truth, and is interested only in its own not very secret agenda. But the media, by and large, are even farther removed from Christian values than is the Church from the values of the media.

The discrepancy starts quite far back. As I said, the media

do not normally pretend to be in business for the purpose of 'doing good'. They do not make a very loud claim to any part in the process of social engineering, and if they proselytise for values that may or may not be Christian this is usually in the form of a short-term campaign, which is always ancillary to the paper's or the television station's commercial purposes. We should remember from the start that this is the world of Mammon not God. All Human Life is There: and the bottom line is not always enhanced by the search for a Civilisation of Love.

On the other hand, the underlying value-system proclaimed by the media does have something in common with the Christian. I shall refer mainly to the press, and the trend-setters in these matters, the tabloid press. At the leading edge of any debate about values, it is actually the tabloids that matter most. Television may be watched by more people, especially by more children, and it is without much doubt the most potent medium through which to convey a message. It is, I guess, the subject most people think of when they talk about the power of the media. But one of the features of television in this country is that it is discussed almost to death, and exists within a regulatory régime which ensures that the debate about its performance is both continuous and influential. There may be a great deal of pap and innocuous rubbish filling the hours of day and night, but argument at the controversial borderlines – whether about violence, or taste or political balance – is intense and constant and public, and is one to which publishers and producers are finely sensitised. By and large, it produces a television output which may pander to materialism and instant pleasure and other secular transgressions, but rather seldom glories in outrage or boasts about its latest violation of the norms of decency. Here it is the tabloids that are changing the culture, with television and the rest of us in the press drawn at least into reflecting them and sometimes, remorselessly, into following them down the slope. While the appearance of a four-letter word on prime-time television provokes outraged tabloid headlines, the tabloids' own daily indulgence in lies, brutal unfairness and petty obscenity passes unexamined: treasured, even, as a pillar of the national heritage with almost as long a pedigree as the Tower of London.

As I say, they do not seriously pretend to be promoting Christianity, but certain familiar premises underline their work. Behind every tabloid outing of an errant MP, there's the presumption that he should be obeying the code of a normal Christian gentleman. Every judge or priest or teacher who lapses from grace in any way, and is punished under the lash of a *Sun* headline, is being faced with the implicit existence of a behavioural norm – sometimes professional but usually moral – from which they have regrettably departed. Somewhere inside the tabloid universe is a complete ethical system, of which the editors are the guardians, which sets the standards everyone must meet or face condign vengeance on behalf of the citizenry at large: that is, the tabloid reader, whose interest in the bonking politician, the negligent mum, the thieving bank manager, the once-again bonking actress, is fuelled only by a common awareness that these things should not happen.

The tabloids, in other words, set themselves up high. So do other newspapers, though with a different menu of crimes. But it's the tabloids who trade most relentlessly in the coin of hypocrisy, and bring to their transactions the most ruthless ways of dealing; they who demand the right to intrude and invade, to damage and destroy, in what they will always call, if pushed to justify themselves, the public interest. Why, you might even believe that selfless concern for the wider community, its right to know and its interest in an ordered society, is what really drives the tabloid press.

But let's measure this not according to Christian values

but, as is often instructive, by the opposite test. How intimately does the tabloid press cohabit with the seven deadly sins? Here, perhaps, we see the outlines of a real Satanic pact.

First comes pride. Should we speak here of the bottomless vanity of these newspapers' self-importance? Or perhaps of the empty nationalism they stoke up, raving against Europeans, unleashing lager louts across the continent before railing against them when they smash up innocent towns while wrapped in the Union Jack? Wrath is ever-present, fury and anger being the only means of which politicians, in the tabloid world, are capable. *Envy*: where would they be without the daily pabulum of other people's lives, the wistful looking through the window, the yearning for homes and life-styles that will be for ever out of reach? Lust? I need say nothing about lust, except that of all the seven it is beyond doubt the first among equals, the one sin without which the tabloid world would collapse. Gluttony is less of a danger than it was when the Bible was composed, diet books have taken over as the key spring-time remedy for falling tabloid sales. But Avarice is faithfully upheld at all times, the motor of the acquisitive society without which the economics of all journalism would be at risk. As for Sloth, the last of the seven, it is the very description of what tabloid reading is about: nasty, brutish and short, built on the pretence that no event is too complex to be absorbed by the idle perusal of two hundred staccato words.

Actually, when I think about these sins, they do not all seem very sinful. Newspapers that commit them might be described as reflecting the competitive, progressive, leisured, innocently pleasure-seeking society Britain has become in the late twentieth century. But there are traits in the tabloid press performance which seem to me worth scrutinising through the Christian prism, and which, thus refracted, are seen to make nonsense of their high claims:

above all, their claim to be the scourge of hypocrisy wherever it is found.

The first of these is cruelty. Again I accept that the tabloids are not alone. Grey and broadsheet print is as capable of cruel effect as the lurid screaming downmarket. The latest fashion in television is for the dramatised portrayals of recent human tragedies, in which living people of no public importance are depicted against their will by actors re-enacting a murder case or other crime. This causes endless misery to a few people, while giving voyeuristic pleasure to the millions without a single grain of the public interest, in the proper sense, being at stake. It is meant to be believed as fact, while any deviations from fact are treated as legitimate dramatic licence. The justifications the television companies offer for these acts of opportunistic exploitation treat the feelings of completely innocent people with contemptible disdain.

But in the tabloid world, cruelty is an unconsidered trifle: the residual over-matter from search-and-destroy exercises that scorch the earth and take no hostages. That's what characterised the treatment of the Prince and Princess of Wales through many years of their unhappy marriage. If by-standers, like children, got in the way, too bad. If yet another half-baked revelation was certain to make the misery deeper, too bad again. It's the same with other public figures. Beside the inadequately held debate about privacy and press intrusion, there's the even less acknowledged question of how far people's feelings matter. I feel embarrassingly unfashionable to raise it now. But don't forget: these newspaper do lay claim to high ground. Every time they pay some tramp to kiss and tell, they cobble together a justification locating the sordid material not in the commercial interest but the public interest. They affect to be standing up for a sinless world, where every public figure is a straight arrow. Yet their own public performance is saturated in the hypocrisy which it is their stock-in-trade to condemn in everybody else.

Second, what view of human nature do they convey? Almost invariably the lowest. Sentimental paeans to heroic life-savers, gallant policemen, tireless grannies, saintly and giving entertainers are, of course, part of the commercial mix. Brave Brits rescuing Spanish donkeys or adopting Bosnian orphans are part of the stuff of tabloid Britain. But the dominant note is of ridicule and contempt. I am the last person to yearn for newspapers of good news. Nobody wants to buy them, and they try, absurdly, to redefine what news is. News is, for the most part, the news of failure not triumph, of human shortcomings rather than decencies. The exception to this are the sports pages, the last refuge of the journalism of the flawless hero, something we all like to read from time to time. Otherwise, day by day, the tabloids find it hard to rise above the journalism of the common denominator at its lowest. And again, the Christian perspective asks a question. Does man, or woman, need to be portrayed in colours of such unrelenting coarseness?

Third, I come back to the question of truth. I've said the Church has problems with this, but so do sections of the press. Within truth I encompass not just accuracy but such qualities as fairness and honesty. I think that within the format, tabloids sometimes try not to be exactly inaccurate. They are sometimes reckless, but usually take care to avoid being disprovable on the precise details. But as for honesty, still less fairness, the entire tabloid mode, with its emphasis on instant effect and maximum shock-value, runs counter to those objectives. One only has to consider the reporting of politics in the *Sun*, the *Star*, the *Express* and the *Mail* to see that even-handed fairness exists nowhere in their codes of conduct. But I would stretch this farther. Since fairness is often dull, and the value-free inquiry into truth often painstaking, it doesn't have much of a chance among newspapers whose interest, above all, is in winning the circulation war.

Competition, indeed, is at the heart of a lot of this, and not just in the tabloid press. But the downward pressure of competition on journalistic quality, an object lesson that runs hard against the culture of the hour and the decade, is a subject for another day. On this occasion I am addressing the Christian theme, and am conscious that I have shown no overflowing excess of the Christian virtue of optimism. I say nothing of the Church's faith, but if the tabloids have no charity, can I muster any hope?

First, the Church. The Church, I'm sure, considers that it is fighting a losing battle for the values it stands for in face of media which, for all their pretensions, are fundamentally not interested in promoting them. It does certain things to stake out some ground. It has defended, quite rightly, the small but massively listened to God-slot, *Thought for the Day*, on the BBC *Today* programme on Radio 4. Why on earth the propagation of the atheist position should command equal time with this tiny religious moment in an otherwise godless medium was always unclear to me. The Church – the Churches – also spend time and money preparing their leaders to make the right impression on television on those rare occasions when they are given the chance to do so. They have communications sub-sections that study media output and make suggestions for how these might be judged and improved by Christian standards. The mainstream Churches, moreover, have become quite sophisticated in their approach, getting away from simplistic homilies about sex and violence. But I sense that they feel a waning of confidence. And who can say they are mistaken? The media do not find the propagation of Christian values very helpful to their commercial interest.

My suggestion for the Church, especially the Catholic Church, however, is to accept a greater challenge. I think that, to serve media values at their highest, the Church needs to develop a different approach to secular truth. If it did this, its under-regarded preaching in favour of eternal moral verities might be more widely attended.

It needs to be more open, and more honest. It should accept that the serious reporting of its institutional history, the complexities and the frailties alike, is a legitimate task which it does not have the right to manipulate and control in the way, everywhere from Rome to Dublin, it still, by second nature, tries to do. The time has surely come when enquiring into the truth about the institutions need not be equated with contesting the truth of the faith. The Church has still to find the grammar, and perhaps the psychology, that would permit it to engage with the truth-seeking and truth-telling purposes of responsible and independent journalism. It still has a top-to-bottom attitude which, on questions of faith and morals, the world is ready – indeed, increasingly delighted – to listen to, but which, on history and politics and money and self-regulation and the other concerns that are common to all the institutions of this world, does it no good. The Church has a big problem with honesty and truth. Its instinct is still for silence and the cover-up.

The confession of error is something it demands of its adherents, but not of itself, as we have seen, for example, in the sad story about the Cardinal Archbishop of Vienna. I think it could set a better example, without the walls of the kingdom tumbling down.

For the media, and especially the tabloids I've been talking about, realignment is more difficult to imagine. But there is something deeply flawed about their attitude to themselves and the world which deserves to be more stringently exposed – not least by the custodians of Christian values on the other side of the aisle.

At the heart of the newspapers' contract with society are

questions of responsibility. In this ethical system which, I've suggested, even the tabloids construct a matrix within which all people can be tested and found wanting, and responsibility is a key component. It's the failure of the politician, the judge, the general, the bishop, to live up to the responsibilities they've taken on that opens them to the opprobrium of the *Sun*. They've fallen down on their standards, and deserve everything they get.

Well, the newspaper industry has standards too, and a body to enforce them, the Press Complaints Commission. This has made a valiant effort to write a code of proper journalistic practice, largely to ward off the threat of statutory regulation. It has been moderately successful; complaints about intrusions into privacy, especially, have gone down But that is not my point now. The point is that the PCC represents the affirmation by the industry as a whole that it, too, has a sense of responsibility; not, perhaps, that in a churchly way it wants to do good, but that it recognises objective standards which it is its job to live up to.

What I find least forgivable about the press's psychology, but especially that of the tabloids, is the willingness in practice to disclaim that personal or institutional responsibility and replace it with something quite different – namely the responsibility of their own readers. The fact that people buy the papers, these editors glibly trot out, is enough to settle the matter: game, set and match to the pedlars of cruelty and purveyors of dishonest anti-truth. Suddenly this is supposed to answer all the questions. Even to the point of highest professional acclaim. The other day, at the British Press Awards, the moment when the industry makes a decision about which words, of all the millions written in a year's journalism, deserve the prize, the judges chose to garland one reporter who'd scooped the pool on Camilla Parker-Bowles's divorce, and another who'd done a number under the headline 'Di's Cranky Phone calls to Married Oliver'. The industry, represented by all the papers, solemnly declared that the *News of the World* was almost the newspaper of the year, surpassed only by the *Daily Mail*.

It's even worse than that. Outside the industry as well, the journalism of cruelty and lies is regarded with a typically British respect. Ministers don't like the privacy invasions, and politicians don't like their colleagues being caught in the wrong bed. But there's a ghastly sense in which the *Sun* is treated as a kind of national treasure, its outrageous headlines cherished, its dig-in-the-ribs sauciness the talk of the chattering classes. Mobilised every four years to help win an election, these skills have brought the Tories rich reward, which perhaps accounts for the official tolerance of their excesses. Why aren't the tabloids subjected to a tenth of the angst that permeates attitudes to television? There are many reasons, but one of them surely has to do with their mighty power to keep the governing party in thrall to their demands.

There may not be much that can be done about this. I'm not in favour of more censorship or a privacy law. But I am in favour of making the tabloids outcasts. Politicians should not write for them, television and radio shouldn't report them, other papers shouldn't humour, still less reward them. Columnists like Woodrow Wyatt, attacking the *News of the World* from one Murdochian pulpit in *The Times*, should be excoriated as a hypocrite for none the less continuing to take the Murdoch shilling as a columnist who brings all the respectability of the House of Lords to another column in, yes you've guessed it, the *News of the World*. That kind of double standard is what I mean by the tabloids being at the sharp edge of moral and cultural decline.

But the worst of it finally is their willingness to absolve themselves from any form of accountability for their output. Insisting that ministers keep to standards, how do the tabloids get away with sub-contracting their own? You could call it, if you were charitable, the apotheosis of the market philosophy in which the British have been re-inducted over the last fifteen years. As long as people want it, anything goes. But that's what Stanley Baldwin said about the harlot throughout the ages: power without responsibility. It is, for these pious invigilators of everyone else's behaviour, the ultimate hypocrisy, eating its way into the culture, leaving hardly anyone untouched. At bottom it says that because this is no longer an actively Christian society, decent Christian values are no longer the responsibility of the people with the greatest power to cherish and protect them. I have a headline for Murdoch and his editors: On Your Knees!

Rt Hon John Patten MP

Former Secretary of State for Education

John Patten was born in 1945. He was educated at Wimbledon College and Sidney Sussex College, Cambridge, and is a Fellow of Hertford College, Oxford. In 1976 he published *The Conservative Opportunity* with Lord Blake and has published a number of other books and articles. He was first elected as Member of Parliament when he won the City of Oxford seat from Labour in the General Election of May 1979.

Appointed Parliamentary Private Secretary to Ministers of State at the Home Office in 1980, Mr Patten became Parliamentary Under Secretary of State for Northern Ireland in January 1981 and served until 1983.

He contested the new seat of Oxford West and Abingdon after redistribution in June 1983. Following that election, he was appointed Parliamentary Under Secretary of State, Department of Health and Social Security, as Junior Health Minister, and in September 1985 transferred to the Department of the Environment as Minister of State and Minister for Housing, Urban Affairs and Construction.

Following the June 1987 General Election he became Minister of State at the Home Office and in January 1990 was made a Privy Counsellor. After the 1992 Election Mr Patten was appointed Secretary of State for Education, a post from which he resigned in the Cabinet reshuffle of July 1994. In 1995 he published *Things To Come. The Tories in the 21st Century,* and is now Adviser to the Board of Charterhouse Bank in the City of London.

Rt Hon John Patten MP
Christian Values in Education

It may not be surprising that John Patten, having
been educated by tough-minded nuns, and then even
tougher-minded Jesuits, firmly believes in the *teaching*
of moral values to children from an early age within
the framework of the family. He re-examines the case
for Christian values being taught to our children on
the eve of a new millennium.

4

I have just two overriding but interlinked themes. The *first* is that Christian values should be central to education in a Christian country, while respecting all other faiths and beliefs from Judaism and Islam to Hinduism.

The *second* is that those Christian values, besides informing the lives of children under the influence of preachers and the instruction of teachers, are also vital to the development of that common mechanism which now links countries and communities across the globe of all religions and none – the market. The market needs to be regulated, but vigorous capitalism provided it has its own strong moral component is something which is a positive good, if put to good uses. It should be thus recognised, taught and praised by Christians and others, both from the pulpit and in the classroom.

If we should, rightly, have a bias to the poor and need constantly to be reminded of our duty of charity, then those who by their labour and at all levels create wealth – which helps to pay for the support of the needy – must have their positive, practical and moral contributions recognised. Yet I simply cannot remember in my adult life ever hearing such a message from the pulpit, whether in the Cathedral – where we have worshipped when in London since 1978 – or elsewhere. This sometimes seemingly fastidious attitude by the clergy (high and low), who are quite rightly ready when necessary to condemn statesmen and politicians, greedy business men and crooked financiers, for their failings, is likely only to marginalise those who deserve some notice for their efforts.

So we need, to put it mildly, a clear and non-relativist lead from Christianity's leaders – whether of the cloth or not – about the importance of religious education. But we also need the help of this religious education in order to underpin a reborn theology of work which in its turn can be a foundation for the moral legitimacy of the free market. We are all free market men and women now, more or less, world wide – with some exceptions. In the UK today, all political parties espouse the market as the most desirable economic system. Ownership is a simple fact not only of our economic life but of our social organisation. In the United Kingdom, because of our history, we need naturally to look at the problems of capitalism first through Christian-tinted spectacles. Business ethics need their advocates. The Jewish Association for Business Ethics shows how this can be done. Until I began to write this a few months ago, and enquired 'Is there a similar Christian organisation?' I had not, I am ashamed to say, heard of a body called The Christian Association of Business Ethics despite the fact that it was launched over fifty years ago as The Catholic Industrialists' Conference (becoming ecumenical only after Vatican II). Its mission of undertaking dialogue with the Churches, to interpret business activity as a human response to God's commands to renew the face of the earth and to undertake the creation and re-creation of wealth as part of the process of building God's Kingdom on earth, is a dialogue worth having with politicians too. Although I have been in Parliament for sixteen years, ignorant of its existence and doubtless very valuable work, its mission is certainly a 'dialogue' worth having with teachers as well as politicians.

Why this stress on the thoroughly unfashionable and, to many, uncomfortable-sounding word 'capitalism'? It is because ownership supports family life, helps to make men and women free, and keeps the state in its box. Mgr Gilbey is surely right when he writes in his masterly *We Believe*[1] that

the root of the idea of property is the material security that a family needs to fulfil its continuing obligation. The state should guarantee to parents the peaceful possession of what they justly own. The family and the concept of property are both profoundly moral concepts, very closely interlinked.

That there is clear papal authority for these words is plain to me. It is contained in this quotation:

Property and other forms of private ownership of external goods contribute to the expression of personality and provide man with the opportunity of exercising his role in society and in the economy; it is very important, then, that the acquisition of some form of ownership of external goods by individuals and communities be fostered. Private property or some form of ownership of external goods assures a person a highly necessary sphere for the exercise of his personal and family autonomy and ought to be considered as an extension of human freedom. Lastly, in stimulating the exercise of responsibility, it constitutes one of the conditions for civil liberty.

Now, you might think, precisely which reactionary nineteenth-century Pope or dictator-dealing twentieth-century Pope, am I praying in aid of these ideas? Maybe it is Pius IX who so notably declared that the Church had no need to come to terms with the liberalism of the nineteenth century? Or perhaps the later Pius XI, at the time when he was making concordats with the dictators between the two World Wars? No, neither of these popes, for it is rather an extract from one of the documents of the Second Vatican Council, *Gaudium et Spes*, section 71, which guide us today.

Why do I feel so strongly about these two issues? Because, *first*, while I think what differentiates us from the animals is our having been born with some moral sense, morality and virtue do need to be fearlessly taught to the young. This should not be done in a hand-wringing or relativist way. *Second*, I think this is vital because that morality itself must inform capitalism, which now shapes all our worlds. It should do this in at least two ways: by providing the framework of trust and honesty within which business should operate, and by providing guidance on what should be done with wealth once acquired, such as in the matter of charitable endeavour.

It is both patronising and profoundly uncharitable to suggest that because businessmen and women run international or domestic businesses in order to make money, that they are somehow of lesser value in God's eyes, or in our national secular scheme of things. So, morality matters both in itself and in relation to capitalism. The young should be *taught* it. Why? I turn next to the Chief Rabbi at whose feet I freely admit to find myself sitting, for guidance. He, like his predecessor, Lord Jakobovitz, speaks with bell-like clarity and in an unembarrassed way on these matters, just as spiritual leaders should. In his book published a little earlier this year called *Faith in the Future*, he writes:

Morality matters. Not just because we seek to be judgemental or self-righteous or pious ... It matters because we care for liberty, and have come to understand that human dignity is better served by the restraints we impose on ourselves than those forced upon us by external laws and punishment and Police ... Morality matters because we believe that there are other and more human ways of living than instinctual gratification tempered by regret.

He goes on:

> Morality matters, finally, because despite all fashionable opinion to the contrary, we remain moved by altruism. We are touched by other people's pain. We feel enlarged by doing good, more so perhaps by doing *well*, by material success. Decency, charity, compassion, integrity, faithfulness, courage, just by being there for other people matter to us.

And ends:

> These Truths, undervalued for a generation, are about to become vital again.[2]

The Chief Rabbi is quite right. His book should be widely read by all, just as Roman Catholics would benefit from the close and continuing study of *We Believe*, which concentrates on reflecting the simple but profound messages of the old 'penny' catechism.

Morality needs to be taught. What is it? Morality is simply about the distinction between right or wrong, or good and evil, in relation to actions and character. It is critical for educators to strive to put flesh on these abstract qualities. They are underpinned by values which we all recognise, if we are not frightened to say so.

So, for the good of the coming generation, and for the moral functioning of the market economies in which they will undoubtedly live, it is vital that these sorts of value are taught by us to our children. Such values are timeless. They are the very basis of our lives. I am not suggesting a return to some out-of-date idea that no one takes seriously now. I am, however, convinced that there is far more widespread support for these basic values than the cynics would have us believe, and that relativism might well have run its late twentieth-century course, having reached a post-1960s peak, which has done much damage.

Education comes first. Values must lie at the heart of education. No school should be a value-free zone. Every school must have its own ethos, underpinned by a shared sense of values. These inform everything that happens, in the classroom, in the school corridor, the playground or staff room. They should be recognised by everyone in the community of the school, pupils, staff, parents, governors.

Values need to be taught, deliberately, seriously and explicitly. Why? Because we are all born with propensities of various sorts which can be positive or negative, and which need directing in the right way. The doctrine of original sin is a profound truth. Good schools (and good parents!) recognise this. Religious instruction as such, of course, takes place only in religious schools – Christian, Jewish, Muslim and others. But Christian values (which are, as it happens, the ethical values for other religions too) are those which should be the norm in the generality of non-demoninational, maintained British schools, respecting minorities and ensuring that Christian children have a good understanding of other faiths.

Religious education must always avoid two things. First, it should never be a matter of unthinking *religious indoctrination* even when delivered by priests, nuns and other holy people as part of legitimate *religious instruction* in denominational schools. Religious *instruction*, in that denominational sense, should not by law be given in non-denominational schools. There is a clear distinction between the religious instruction that one might receive in a church or as a convert, and the properly more detached religious education appropriate to a non-denominational school.

But, second, the other side of the coin is that religious education must not relax into the soft option of teaching comparative religion – that somehow religious education is just about Lent and Ramadan, Diwali and Channukah. It should be about very much more than a value-free approach summed up by the line of thinking 'isn't it all *so* interesting, children, we *do* live in a very diverse world, don't we, and this is how different people do their religion.' Children should certainly have some education in these things, but that is no substitute for a type of religious education which takes care not to relax into seeing religion and morality as facets of anthropology, but rather which stresses the centrality of Christianity in our national life and history, and as the basis of our shared morality. To suggest otherwise would be an intellectual cop-out of the first order. That is why proper assemblies in school are so important.

British religious education, informed by our historic Judaeo-Christian tradition, had better be the reference point, starting with the foundation stone of the firm teaching of the principles of morality for our children. To do this, through beginning the long and difficult task of explaining why morality matters, does not mean telling pupils exactly what they should do in every conceivable circumstance. It does, however, mean helping them to draw from their basic moral values a clear set of attitudes and rules of conduct which are compatible with the way in which they and we would wish to live.

It is vital that such religious education explains that values are an expression of a deeper truth beyond, and less ephemeral than, our material lives, that they provide ideals for us to live up to, that if we sometimes fail, it is no excuse for not trying, indeed that is a spur for trying to do better.

This is beautifully reflected by the monks of Ampleforth (who did not educate me; the Jesuits at Wimbledon had that task), who published in 1993 *St Benedict's Prayer Book for Beginners*.[3] Tough stuff this, particularly the quotations at the foot of each page from the Rule of St Benedict – cheery exhortations like 'live in fear of judgment day' or 'have a great horror of hell' (let alone the one which I find most difficult of all, 'do not pamper yourself'). It is not, however, those particular gobbets from the Rule which strike me most, but rather the quotation on the frontispiece of the volume which is so telling: 'Always we begin again.' This is no bad motto for those bearing the considerable burdens of teaching religion, and having to explain that simply because living by a moral checklist or set of moral tenets is beyond most of us for every moment of every day, that does not mean that we should not *try*.

It is only from realising this that pupils will come to appreciate that values are also necessary conditions for a civilised community, that their possession is its very hallmark. The ownership of a set of values which give meaning to life – and guide action – is a characteristic of people of all faiths and of none. If it should be clear that we need a set of shared values so that we can live harmoniously together, then it must be triumphantly true that we also face chaos if we fail to instil such essential attributes.

I have a list of those core values to which all sorts of believers – and unbelievers – should cleave.

- A recognition that there is such a thing as morality.
- Acceptance of responsibility.
- Self-discipline and self-reliance.
- Unselfishness and the need for self-restraint.
- Loyalty and fidelity.
- Honesty and trustworthiness.
- Courtesy and respect for the views of others.
- Regard for proper authority.

Such values are difficult and are not just absorbed effort-lessly by children. They need to be taught with deliberation – and without fear. This is no easy task. In an age when the prevailing ethos among the chattering classes is still that the absolute must be politically incorrect, and where 'relativism rules OK' is still scrawled on the walls of a few teacher-training colleges, the challenge is brisk.

At a time when we are told by social analysts of every hue from left to right that family values are not now formed and transmitted as they might be, particularly where there are no fathers (or what are known in the sociological trade as 'male role models'), then school is the sole stage to which at least some of our children must look for some thoroughly modern – not mediaeval nor Victorian – morality plays to help guide them. Schools act as microcosms of the different communities in which pupils will eventually take their places. It is in school that children should begin to learn how to live out the values and expectations necessary both for them and their communities to function properly.

From this overall approach to education in values at school should flow the development of a positive attitude to learning, and a 'can-do' approach to life in general. Whether children grow up and choose to be believer or atheist, Green, Liberal, Socialist, Tory or flat-earther, they should be imbued with an enduring respect for rational argument, for the legitimate interests of others, and for the views and customs of different groups in different communities. This should promote in each child a sense of fair play which is carefully mixed with independence of thought. It should also engender an enterprising approach to meeting challenges coupled with persistence at working at solutions that make achievement possible. Such an approach, and such personal and *disciplined* achievements, are as vital in the young charity worker in the Third World as they are to the young derivatives trader in the City of London.

Thanks to assembly-line workers and the providers of services, as well as a myriad of others who work to create wealth, we all have the ability to plan our own lives (and those of our children) and to help others. These are a great moral good. Thus, capitalism is a force for good: its profits pay for the things modern communities wish to see their citizens enjoy. Capitalism, too, must be underpinned by a firm morality.

Capitalism must not float unanchored in a moral vacuum. The moral arguments for the market economy are founded in the freedom and prosperity that is engendered by it. To say this does not mean that the financier is in any sense better – or for that matter worse – than the nurse. They have their own roles and values. But the latter could not function without the former, and vice versa. Both those working not-for-profit, and those working for profit, can be bad. Just because a financier is caught with his or her hand in the till does not mean that all financiers are bad, and therefore that capitalism is evil. Equally, the occasional serial killing nurse (whom we have seen in recent years) does not signify that the whole profession of nursing is thus tainted. Nor does the occasional adulterous or child-molesting priest (and we have seen them as well) mean that all men of the cloth are a potential danger to the young.

All in all, I have *always* found must businessmen and businesswomen very straightforward compared with other classes in the community. They work hard to make money by making or trading things, and/or providing services. This is often a very single-minded matter, demanding much drive, application and mental endeavour. Most businessmen and businesswomen pay their taxes and are deeply law-abiding. Many are equally deeply (and *quietly*) involved in charitable activity which takes their time and money. They set business targets, and drive openly towards them. Most are much less prone to the compromises and pettinesses that often run through political or academic life (both of which I also know intimately) or Church life and journalism (both of which I have observed closely). It is my experience that, along with farmers and soldiers, business people usually have an almost entirely unembarrassed straightforwardness to their characters in their professional lives.

They also need regular supplies of new blood in the shape of the boys and girls that leave our schools to work for them. Thus while a well-ordered business world has a lot to give to the creation of well-organised and functioning communities, it also depends on them. The business world wants a stable and orderly country where things work. They want to make the money which helps to make things work – they also need well-educated people to do the job.

Just as the business world needs supplies of new and well-qualified young people, so also should they keep their own moral frameworks in good order. We need a clear, modern theology of work to underpin the free market. The legitimacy of free markets depends on the firmest ethical foundations. This is very hard to legislate for. We can devise all the laws, regulators and supervisory bodies imaginable, but if there is not a firm ethical culture of and for capitalism (substantially derived from the set of values that I have already listed) then much will be lost. There can, by comparison, be magnificently worded Bills of Rights to ensure the constitutional safeguards for citizens, but without the culture of freedom such Bills mean nothing. This was, for example, the case in the old USSR from the 1920s – and in its many satellites from the late 1940s until their collapse in the late 1980s. Paper rights without a supportive political culture are meaningless. In exactly the same way, regulatory edifices will be found to be made of straw if they are not embedded within an ethical culture that consciously supports capitalism.

Capitalism above all else should serve. Neither service nor integrity are antipathetic to the capitalist ethic. These characteristics are rather essential to capitalism. This will be all the more so in our knowledge-based and service-driven economies in the coming decades, for suddenly goods can be made to a very high standard of once unimaginable quality, but by very few people. Now so much of the profit in business is in the design, the follow-up, the warranties, the services given, the care and maintenance – and not just in making of mechanical parts or the act of selling a financial bond. Service is critical to capitalism. So is morality. Capitalism is not simply about meeting human needs and helping human happiness, nor keeping the state necessarily in its box before it gets the chance to dehumanise communities, families and individuals. It also bestows freedom on men and women. Thus far I have quoted a monsignor, a chief rabbi, and a community of holy monks, all of whom have written books, all of which are sold for profit, and doubtless put to different ends, having employed a myriad of talented people to these purposes. Capitalism is thus about freedom, just as freedom is critical to it, that freedom to buy and sell your service, your goods, your ideas, your creativities, your religious thoughts.

What children and young people need to be taught is that capitalism is also about an expression of 'my will and my responsibilities' leading them to understand that work is a good thing, not just because it produces the wherewithal to live, but because it is a social phenomenon as well. 'Capitalism', 'the market economy', whatever you choose to call it, is about people freely exchanging and freely contracting, and accepting the consequent costs and responsibilities. It therefore has a strong social component. Capitalism is not just the oil on the wheels of the economy, it is a vital lubricant in the social mechanisms of country, community, family and individual life. It needs a clearly understood framework with a strong moral component.

This should be reflected, I think, partly in religious education lessons as such, and partly also in the general run of instruction under the heading of 'other subjects' where none the less valuable lessons about life can be imbued. It is vital for teachers to make their pupils aware of the moral challenges and necessities of capitalism, for this is the world that their charges will enter. It is also, of course, good for teachers to remind themselves that it is through the profits of other taxpayers that their salaries are paid – just as those 'other taxpayers' should be aware and remember that the products of those teachers are vital to the supply side of the economy. Given no bright, hard-working, ambitious and achieving youngsters, the free market would soon collapse. We should be grateful to teachers that this does not happen.

There is nothing wrong with men and women prizing success – some saints have done this. But in the drive for the success of an economic system on which the whole apparatus of our modern community depends, it must never be forgotten that this should not be morally neutral. It should try always positively to encourage the good and discourage the bad. If it does not do this, then capitalism will indeed be the pig philosophy against which Carlyle warned.[4]

Some, even today, might say, 'But surely this is a doctrine about personal benefit?' The quick answer is easy – no capitalism and no production, no wages and no charity. It is possible, simply for the sake of argument, to go a bit deeper, however.

What of the parish priest or holy nun? Are they sacrificing their lives just for God and the community – or also for the pursuit of heavenly salvation (i.e. for their own benefit)? You can erect an argument which would suggest that there are in fact no altruistic professions or callings which do not also provide mental and spiritual benefits. Take the nurse: is his or her reward only reasonable pay? What about the approval of society, the appreciation of patients, the comforting and self-satisfied sense of having people dependent on you? Indeed, does helping other people simply make you feel better about yourself, and in your secret moments rather superior too? Uncomfortable questions? Perhaps, but they must be answered, particularly by those who shed patronising scorn from the moral high ground which they have assumed for themselves, while very often living on resources generated by others.

It can be exactly the same with self-styled 'public servants' who have assumed positions of considerable authority through controlling (or some would say interfering with) the private activities of others. Society's plaudits have often been richly deserved by such men and women, though sometimes the honours, public attention and social importance have also seemed to me of considerable personal value to these unelected people, with the infinite job security and later immense potential to earn while lecturing or writing about their experiences.

Nurses, priests and nuns, great public servants, are all involved professionally in loving their neighbours – healing the sick, helping other human beings in distress, looking after those who cannot look after themselves. But that is not all that 'loving your neighbour' means. What it should also mean is wanting your neighbour to have the chance to follow their own freely-chosen purposes. In other words, what we want above all else for ourselves, and what we should strive to accord to our neighbour, is that freedom to pursue our own purposes within the law of the land, and under God's law. That is what capitalism is really about, operating on the basis of respect for free, independent and responsible persons – that freedom and independence, that responsibility and opportunity to take your own risks and bestow your own charity, once having been the preserve of the rich and the mighty, is now within the grasp of many. Thus, capitalism may not be perfect, but it is certainly morally mature and deserves to be properly explained to the young.

How should that be done? It is through explaining the following five key features of a moral market economy:

- promises being made and kept
- contracts honoured
- responsibilities acknowledged
- duties undertaken
- individuality respected.

There is also an essentially human component, and that is found in the fiscal aspect of capitalism. Payment in a market system means something, for it is a recognition of human endeavour, a decision to buy something of quality, or obtain a valued service. Payment is therefore not seen as being just about money doled out by an inhuman state, or something of value which may be eroded by inflation or otherwise wasted.

There is something much more than this, as well, which is entirely human. Capitalism makes generosity, both of a financial sort and that which depends on personal endeavour, possible in the first place.

Above all, the young must be taught that business is part of the natural social order. Its purpose is to meet human needs by making and distributing goods and services in an efficient manner. Thus how this is done is important to us all. They must also understand that competition between businesses is a good thing. It has always been the way that resources are not wasted, prices are kept fair and costs minimised. At the same time, they must equally be taught that the state has a duty to see that markets operate fairly and competition is maintained – business must not frustrate this. Above all else, that private enterprise has the potential to make efficient and sustainable use of resources, creating wealth for the benefit of all. Today, employees entering work expect clear statements of their terms and conditions, benefits and facilities. I should like to see a clear and simple statement of business ethics given to them too, just as I should like to read such issues addressed rather more in company annual reports than hitherto.

Capitalism powers the gentler arts, makes it possible for the active citizen to be even more active, and the liberty which it bestows gives all of us the opportunities that were once there only as the proud prerogatives of the very rich, for the majority of us are able now to be charitable of our time and money if we choose. This is probably one of its greatest moral benefits. Whether in relation to capitalism, or in the much wider and vital sphere of general religious education, however, it is values like those of our Judaeo-Christian tradition which should inform our national life, and the young in particular. They need to be taught fearlessly.[5]

Notes

1 Monsignor A.N. Gilbey *We Believe*, 1st edn (Valetta, 1983), p.209.

2 Dr J. Sachs, *Faith in the Future* (Darton, Longman & Todd, London, 1995).

3 Anon., *St. Benedict's Prayer Book for Beginners* (Ampleforth Abbey Press, Cambridge, 1993).

4 S. Heffer, *Moral Desperado. A Life of Thomas Carlyle* (Weidenfeld & Nicolson, London, 1995)

5 I am most grateful to Professor A. O'Hear, MA, PhD, Honorary Director of the Royal Institution of Philosophy and Editor of *Philosophy* for reading and commenting upon a draft of this chapter.

Sir Philip Dowson CBE PRA

President of the Royal Academy of Arts

Sir Philip Dowson was born in 1924 and grew up in Norfolk. He attended Gresham's School and, after war service in the Navy, he returned to Cambridge to study architecture. He was a partner of the Ove Arup Partnership until retirement in 1990 and is still a Consultant to the firm.

Since 1970 he has been a member of the Royal Fine Art Commission, and in 1981 received the Royal Gold Medal for Architecture. In addition he is an Honorary Fellow of Clare College, the Royal College of Art, the Duncan of Jordanstone College of Arts, and the American Institute of Architects. He was also a Trustee of the Royal Botanic Gardens, Kew, from 1983 to 1995.

In 1993 Sir Philip was elected President of the Royal Academy of Arts and has been a Royal Academician since 1979.

Sir Philip Dowson CBE PRA
Christian Values in Architecture

Architecture is an art, a craft and a science, and is the
only art that as human beings we inhabit. Our society
is largely an urban one, and architecture is the clothing
of this society. To design is to predict and to prophesy,
so must be within the province of hope if human values
and aspirations are to be reflected and realised in what
we build.

5

I want to start with two propositions to examine why, I believe, we are where we are now. The first is straightforward: that architecture is the only art that we inhabit – but remembering that ugly houses can make happy homes.

The second proposition is more difficult. Almost a century ago, in 1905, Einstein proposed his general law of relativity and, in 1907, Picasso painted the *Demoiselles d'Avignon* – the first totally changed people's perception of physical reality, and the second their perception of visual reality. In undermining the conventional, they undermined people's security. When Stravinsky's *Rite of Spring* was first performed, it started a riot. During the time since we may have caught up intellectually, but psychologically I believe we have never done so – so we have the nostalgia industry.

After the catastrophe of the First World War there was something of a *tabula rasa* and not only in the arts. There was, though, a will for a new start. It was within this environment that the Bauhaus as a school of design was created in Germany. Walter Gropius gathered round him an extraordinary group of architects, artists and craftsmen who tried to combine and integrate an advanced technology with the arts.

Thrown out by Hitler, the Bauhaus was tragically short-lived. Its members, though, and their work created a huge cultural shift internationally and in England gave birth to a whole generation of buildings in the 1930s which embraced its philosophy.

As a fifteen-year-old schoolboy, I remember, for example, the power and clarity of those haunting white architectural images of houses against pine trees; a purity – white almost for virtue and evergreen for fidelity. This imagery though, while not seeming quite to belong to the real world, carried nevertheless within it somehow a moral purpose, an idealist view, hovering somewhere between aspirations and dreams – a powerful mixture.

After the Second World War there was a new world to reconstruct. And we inherited a Modern Movement in pursuit of social aims within an industrialised society.

I touch synoptically on these times to point my position as a modern architect, trying to interpret a changing technology, but always in human terms: a place always for value in our world of fact.

It is easy to argue that society gets the cities and architecture it deserves and economic considerations pre-empt, to a large extent, the results that all of us deplore; that organisations are too often indifferent to architecture or at least disinclined to accept it until first disinfected by a financial propriety, which merely reflects the attitudes of the 'counting house' rather than a culture. In the meantime, nevertheless, the centres of great cities have been disembowelled. Redevelopment has too often become synonymous with destruction. The scale of buildings has become so large as to be out of reach of ordinary mortals and the inhabitants have become alienated and the places unloved.

The word 'architecture' means the art of building. But architecture is an art, a craft and a science, and on the whole the art has recently been at odds with the science and the craft has been disappearing. I should like to express a view – perhaps a rather old-fashioned one – on the last point which, I believe, is of profound importance.

It is not possible to discuss the subject of architecture

without considering the quality which derives very directly from the materials, crafts, skills and techniques from which it is fashioned. Of the great Renaissance architects, Brunelleschi was trained as a goldsmith, Michelangelo was a sculptor, Giotto, Raphael and Bramante were all painters. In our own century, Le Corbusier was trained as a watch engraver, and Mies – the son of a master mason – was for a while apprenticed as a mason himself. I want, from these examples, to emphasise the 'thinking hand' as an integral part of any apprenticeship which seeks excellence in made things. I put this in the most basic terms on purpose. There is no use being a wheelwright unless the wheels are reasonably round, and under these circumstances it is natural for a personal obligation to develop, if for no other reason than self-respect, which in turn implies a morality. So, I believe the ethical, functional and aesthetic will have a natural affinity as a basis for excellence or, at the highest level, for a work of art.

When one thinks back to the Age of Enlightenment, when the Royal Academy of Arts was founded, one tends to think of London as it was then. London was called by eighteenth-century travellers 'the jewel of Europe'. This city was not designed on the whole by architects – but, generally, by builders working within a tradition. Cities – the greatest works of art of all – represent the physical embodiment of the attitudes and values of their societies – their monuments, their symbolism – as well as the ordinary fabric of city life. Architecture is, indeed, the very clothing of a society. But I want to emphasise that most of these buildings, constituting the fabric of the city, were the result of traditional crafts, aided by pattern books and affected, of course, by the swing of fashion, which in turn stemmed from the great patrons and the few architects who were employed by them.

Leading on from there, I want to make another proposition and illustrate it with a particular example of a very great building – King's College Chapel, Cambridge. It is worth reflecting on the richness that these traditions derived from apparently such simple means, and the manifest delight in materials which they exhibit. Also, recognise the discerning eye and thinking hand of the craftsman, and the *language of construction*, which testified to such a human approach, and at times such a highly sophisticated architectural result. It was an achievement which, to a remarkable degree – and this is my main point – combined a coincidence of thought, feeling, understanding and method. As Leonardo da Vinci remarked, 'When the spirit does not work with the hand, there is no art.'

I give this specific example to explain how a constructional idea can lend weight to, and indeed illuminate, an overriding architectural idea: King's College Chapel – God's house, a permanent building to a permanent concept, and so in stone – was constructed to be as high as possible, with heaven in mind, and with the largest windows to bathe it all in the brilliance of light through stained glass. In Genesis, on the first day God said 'let there be light'. It is the gift of light that is to be celebrated with the huge stained glass windows. This great building sought two ideas: height and light. To meet and to build these architectural ideas, and to give visible shape to their spiritual aspirations, a high stone frame, as slender as possible, had to be constructed. The limiting conditions were on the one hand, the crushing strength of stone, and on the other, the minimum thrust from the stone vault. This required a design that worked towards the minimum mass or matter. Within these limits, the construction of stone block on stone block (there was no tensile material such as steel) leads inevitably and irrevocably to the lightening of the structure as it ascends, until finally the vault is made of the thinnest webs of stone within ribs, which echo the underside of a leaf.

Nature never wastes its materials, and in an organic

structure like this, the principle of minimum material underlines and makes possible the whole design. It is an example, in its time, of the most advanced technology being harnessed to meet these architectural ideas – the highest space with heaven in mind – and the largest windows to bathe it all in the brilliance of a celestial light.

The fundamental idea is a beautiful one, and the construction that makes it possible identifies this idea and releases it and makes it real and come alive. It is architecture: the art of building.

Architecture is also very sensual in the widest interpretation of that word, and the hand remains the direct medium for some of our deepest feelings, involving both security and reassurance.

The simple human gesture – to touch, to feel, to handle – to which the first moulding in any pilgrim church also bears witness, is, I believe, of real significance. Whatever other architectural qualities a building may aspire to possess and pass on, the need to communicate at this elementary level, to welcome and to reassure, is surely self-evident, certainly if Freud's dictum is to hold and the conscious be satisfactorily based upon the subconscious.

In thinking about this problem, I have always been fascinated by large, medieval, monastic buildings which, in spite of their size and many building types, were able in so many ways to maintain a very human scale, with marvellously diverse and structured spaces: chapter house, cloister, great church, refectory, cell. They seemed so eloquently to be able to express their purpose, intensity of use, and appropriate mood and again lend weight to the purposes of each community.

One of the secrets perhaps is that within them there is what I think of as a kind of 'invisible armature' with a shape of its own, which tells a story – a narrative, a matrix that includes circulation and the design of the circulation itself – and which links all the parts and spaces together in a coherent way. Here memory is particularly important. We all experience buildings in memory, and in this way we are helped to understand them and locate ourselves within them. One can only wonder at the achievement of the monastic tradition in this respect which allowed so happily for movement, congregation, reflection and withdrawal. What I have referred to as the 'invisible armature' I have always seen as the element which can prevent the 'part' becoming severed from the 'whole', and so the individual from a sense of belonging. These large and extraordinary buildings recognised and reflected, of course, a very great deal more as well – at times the very soul of their society – and their magic continues to seed the imagination of successive generations.

I should like to offer another example. In the monastery at La Tourette, which is for me Le Corbusier's masterpiece, there is a side chapel with a path that rises between altar tables finally up to a cross – a visual metaphor perhaps for the road to Calvary, but unforgettable – where, in the hands of a great architect, visible shape again is given to spiritual aspirations.

In my life I have been asked to design several large headquarters office buildings with working communities of over a thousand people, and I have drawn quite directly from the monastic tradition. As one would imagine, these headquarters buildings have complicated briefs and raise deep and troubling questions of scale and context, site and so on, and above all, of unity and coherence. Stated simply, I suppose the question is of how to get to grips with the scale of large organisations and to clothe them in civilised surroundings as communities of work.

In these large buildings and in some cases developments of a part of a city, we wanted the inhabitants to possess them and be able to use them in the spirit in which they were designed, to make them their own – places full of human references to which to respond, with all that that implies in helping people to feel more at home in them, and awaken their loyalties.

Finally, to design is to predict and to prophesy, and can never be safe, nor can a culture be sterile. In this situation, an architect has to be an optimist. There can indeed be few attitudes more self-indulgent than uncommitted pessimism, other than perhaps indifference. In having to predict and to prophesy, we have to seek an architecture that is drawn from civilised, human and, therefore, Christian values, and from within the province of hope, an architecture of hope.

This architecture must seek to develop methods that can compete with the pressures of scale and technology of today, and revalue them always in human terms, and in the terms of our Christian tradition and society. It must recognise limiting conditions on both growth and resources, which are proving such powerful advocates. This is bound to infuse our design thinking more and more – energy is a simple example. We have an obligation, a Hippocratic Oath if you like, to be sensitive in using our resources for human purposes, and not to attack our environment but to conserve it, to be used and enjoyed. If this is to be so, then a closer understanding and integration between all those involved in design will be essential to help co-ordinate activities in today's climate of technical proliferation which, while embodying the most advanced technically, will not continue to do so at such social and environmental expense.

The cliché 'clarifying science and mystifying art', with its damaging idea of two cultures, is now, one hopes, old hat. Indeed, it has been mystifying science at the expense of clarifying art from which our cities particularly have been more prone to suffer. It is our conscience, as well as the intuitive response to subjective human feelings that must help to establish a place for 'value in our world of fact'. It is the inner eye, the eye of innocence, of the artist, that is I believe too little valued. Within the rising protest at the impoverishment of our surroundings at present there is implicit the need for this eye – the imagination, the gifts that make us human – and nowhere of course is this more necessary than in the architecture of our cities, the physical clothing of our society.

I should like to close with a quotation from Walter Gropius, the founder of the Bauhaus in the early 1920s:

As custodians we must recover a comprehensive vision of the wholeness of the environment in which we live. In our mechanised society we should passionately emphasise that we are still a world of men, and that man in his natural environment must be the focus of all planning.

J. Stuart Horner
CStJ MD FFPHM FRSH DPH DIH

Chairman, Medical Ethics Committee,
the British Medical Association

Dr Stuart Horner was born in 1932 and educated at Wyggeston Grammar School, Leicester, Birmingham University and the London School of Hygiene and Tropical Medicine.

During his career he has been Deputy Medical Officer of Health and Deputy Principal School Medical Officer for the boroughs of Dewsbury and Croydon, Director of Health and Welfare Services for Hillingdon, and District Medical Officer for Croydon.

Until 1989 he was Director of Community Medicine for Preston Health Authority where he is now Director of Public Health. He was made Visiting Fellow in Medical Ethics by the University of Central Lancashire in 1993.

Dr Horner has been Chairman of the Medical Ethics Committee in the British Medical Association since 1989.

J. Stuart Horner
CStJ MD FFPHM FRSH DPH DIH
Christian Values in Medicine

Dr Horner examines the contribution of Christian values to Medicine through a brief historical review. He considers the progressive secularisation of medical ethics in the United Kingdom during the last thirty years and its consequences both for the practice of Medicine and for the medical profession. He also looks at the contributions which Christians can make to the current debate within the profession about 'core values' in Medicine.

6

In November 1994 an historic meeting took place. For the first time representatives of all the major elements within the profession of Medicine met at BMA House to consider the nature of Medicine and its core values.[1] A few weeks ago the Annual Representative Meeting of the BMA asked its governing Council to update the Hippocratic Oath to which all new doctors and medical students might one day make a public commitment.[2] Straws in the wind? Perhaps. Certainly of no statistical significance. These events may, nevertheless, represent the first objective evidence of widespread unease that the relentless pursuit of medical knowledge and new technology should not proceed in an ethical vacuum.

Criticism of the two most recent editions of the BMA's ethical handbook[3,4] have not focused on the intellectual rigour or content. Instead concern has been expressed that the guidance displays a menu of alternative ethical approaches consistent with contemporary trends but reflecting no clear expression of any value system to which the profession as a whole is committed.[5,6] Perhaps this is realistic. Indeed, the collapse of any moral consensus since the Enlightenment causes Saunders[7] to question whether it is really possible 'for the BMA, given the wide disparity in ethical judgments, to produce a book giving a "party" line'. Much is made of the religious and cultural diversity within the profession as in society as a whole. Such facile explanations ignore the obvious fact that this so-called diversity disguises one single dividing line, that is between those on the one hand who believe in some supreme godhead external to the world of the senses and those who believe only in a world they can personally experience.

Nigel Cameron[8] has documented what he describes as *The New Medicine* in which Western medicine has steadily retreated from any commonly agreed ethical values to a world in which yesterday's unthinkable becomes today's practical reality. The foetus has long since been abandoned. Something seems to have persuaded us that at least until it is theoretically capable of independent life, it is non-human to be disposed of as its creators think best. Those who roundly denounced the Nazi experiments on living human beings as inhuman nevertheless tolerated similar experiments on living foetuses no less inhuman in the pain and distress they may have caused.

Courageous doctors in the United Kingdom and the United States, ostracised by their medical establishments, painstakingly exposed human experimentation of which even the participants were unaware.[9] Similar voices are now being raised over the exposure of fraud in medical research.[10] On the horizon is medically assisted death: let us no longer devalue the term euthanasia to which we all aspire. Already legal in the Northern Territories of Australia and the state of Oregon and tolerated in the Netherlands, it seems a peculiarly utilitarian market orientated response to an ageing population. A civilisation once exemplified by its care and compassion for the weak and the dispossessed sees its doctors increasingly as technicians in the refuse disposal business.

How could such a situation ever have arisen? What has caused such a noble profession to falter in its God-given vocation? Does the Christian Church have any responsibility for the present state of affairs? The Church in Russia has experienced the greatest persecution in Christian history. We have much to learn from those who have been to the gates of hell and who have seen, as the Lord promised, that those gates could not prevail against them.[11] In 1973 a Soviet medical oath was promulgated which contained no reference to the Hippocratic tradition.[12] One of the Russian doctors' first tasks when freedom came was to re-establish a pre-Revolutionary type of Hippocratic ethical code. The nightmare is over. Sanity has returned. Western doctors, apparently unaware how precious their inheritance, continue to ignore the warning signs. Perhaps some things are only precious when they have been lost.

Traditionally doctors have looked to Hippocrates when they have been asked to identify their ethical values. It is extremely doubtful that Hippocrates set out to establish a system of moral values in medicine. In religious terms the Greek civilisation of Hippocrates' day bore striking similarities to our own. A wide range of moral values was tolerated with infanticide, sexual laxity and perversion, slavery and assisted death almost universally accepted. A brilliant teacher, Hippocrates was almost certainly more concerned with wresting control of the healing art away from the Asclepian priests[13] and into the hands of the medical profession itself. It is the tradition of self-regulation for which Western medicine owes its greatest debt to Hippocrates. It is difficult to evaluate the motives of a man who lived over two thousand years ago. Nevertheless many scholars[14] believe that Hippocrates was not advocating a series of disinterested patient-centred values into Medicine but rather giving practical advice to his students about ways in which they might enlarge their practices and therefore personal income. Neither Hippocrates nor one of his students is likely to be the author of the Oath which bears his name. Carrick[15] offers cogent arguments for believing that the Oath probably originated among a small group of doctors dedicated to the protection of life, and probably heavily influenced by the Pythagoreans. Certainly it has shown a remarkably enduring quality.

The impact of emerging Christianity upon the Hippocratic tradition was not the natural symbiosis which is often too readily assumed today. Hippocrates had introduced scientific concepts of disease and this created an inherent tension with Christian concepts based on man's fall from grace. Medicine was regarded as treatment for the body. Philosophy was the treatment for the soul in the ancient world and explains why today priests still are given a 'cure of souls'. Temkin in his book *Hippocrates in a World of Pagans and Christians*[16] documents the ambivalent attitude towards Medicine and Hippocrates in the early Church. Consulting a doctor could be seen as a lack of trust in the healing of Christ. Philo was the first Christian to condemn resort to Medicine but Tatian in AD 155 believed that even taking medicines was wrong. Moreover Christians gradually came to associate the Greek pantheon of gods including Aesculepius with demons. Although the Hippocratic Oath in its pagan form was certainly a major document of medical ethics until at least about the end of the fourth century it did not feature prominently in Christian writings of the early centuries. St Jerome gave advice based on it to a priest.[17] At some uncertain time a Christian paraphrase appeared. Temkin[18] concludes that 'Christian culture needed Hippocratic medicine but it did not need Hippocrates as a culture hero for it had its apostles, its saints and martyrs and its great theologians.'

Galen sought to maintain the scientific method that Hippocrates had advocated but his theories imprisoned the scientific growth of Western medicine for nearly a thousand years. During this period, by common consent, Jewish and Muslim doctors were recognised for their technical skills. The destruction of the ancient Greek and Roman civilisations and the unhappy control of medical experimentation by the Church of Rome led to many centuries of apparent stagnation. Nevertheless,

MacKinney[19] produces impressive evidence of the persistence of Hippocratic ideas in an unbroken line through the early as well as late Middle Ages in a wide variety of centres. The Hippocratic writings themselves were preserved in the monasteries[20] to burst forth again at Salerno in 1231 when the Emperor Frederick II insisted that all its students in Medicine be required to attend lectures on Hippocrates and Galen. The dispersal of knowledge from the sack of Alexandria and then Constantinople spread across Europe and gave birth to that resurgence of knowledge known as the Renaissance. Medicine was no less a beneficiary than other branches of the ancient universities.

Most of the new scientists saw no conflict between their religious faith and the revolutionary scientific discoveries which were being made. This was God's world and discovering some of His secrets and handiwork merely added to its enjoyment. Despite a return to the traditions and practices of the early Church among a number of more radical Protestant groups Christian doctors had no difficulty in reconciling their discoveries about the human body with their religious faith. Such discoveries dealt a mortal blow to Galen's theories, but while his reputation declined that of Hippocrates began to grow.

The influence of Christian doctors and scientists during this period is impressive. Robert Boyle, William Harvey and Thomas Willis are obvious examples, together with two eminent medical practitioners Thomas Brown of Norwich and Thomas Sydenham of London.[21] A Puritan and Parliamentarian, Sydenham was unable to obtain a select fashionable clientele after the Restoration and turned instead to middle income families. This required a very large clinical practice which provided a veritable treasure trove of clinical medicine.[22] He has been dubbed the 'English Hippocrates' and is almost entirely responsible for driving doctors back to the bedside to observe the clinical manifestations of disease.

Thomas Hodgkin, another famous physician who lent his name to a form of lymphoma, applied his Quaker faith to the practice of his medicine and sponsored several social causes at home and abroad.[23]

During the great plague of London members of the Royal College of Physicians were criticised for fleeing the capital[24] even though there was a long established tradition since the time of Hippocrates that treatment of the patient took priority over personal risks. The Hospital Order of Knights of St. John even referred to their patients as 'our lords the sick'. A number of Christian doctors, including John Allin and Nathaniel Hodges, remained in London to treat the sick and become known as 'plague doctors'.[25]

It would be idle to pretend that all doctors were Christians even though many no doubt found it prudent to conceal their agnosticism. By the beginning of the eighteenth century ethical values in medicine had begun to degenerate quite rapidly. There was an excessive preoccupation with matters of appearance and social etiquette – with what Fissell[26] has described as 'innocent and honourable bribes' in a market-led health care system. Indeed Thomas Beddoes believed that the practices of many trained doctors were no better than those of the quacks whom they were only too willing to vilify[27]

'The new scientific outlook of the seventeenth century was one of certainty about the ability of human reason and experience to solve all problems. Impressed by the achievements of the natural scientists in discovering laws of the physical universe, the men of the eighteenth century Enlightenment believed that they could find laws that governed society and human behaviour'.[28] The movement began in France where its most famous spokesperson was Voltaire. It quickly radiated across Europe to Britain. Its social implications were enormous. Attacks on the bigotry of organised religion led to a campaign for toleration. Politically the role of the state was re-evaluated by John Locke in this country, while Adam Smith in Scotland concluded that individuals pursued self-interest in the economic realm and that if they were given unfettered freedom to do so the net effect would serve the good of the entire society.[29]

The Enlightenment was not necessarily a mortal threat to the Christian faith, although in retrospect it often seems so. Suzuki[30] notes that 'In the early eighteenth century ... many eminent physicians explicitly criticised Locke's secularised understanding of the mind and set up a model of the human mind which was other worldly and was quite different from or even diametrically opposed to, Locke's formulation. They did so largely because they wanted to refute monistic materialism and defend the Christian religion ... they were by no means irreligious and materialistic unbelievers who sought alternatives to Christianity. Similarly Hoffmann, a Christian pietist in Halle, Germany, wrote his *Medicus Politicus*, a book of ethics heavily based on his religious belief.[31] Nearly a century later, Thomas Gisborne,[32] a Christian physician, friend of the Anglican evangelicals including William Wilberforce and a vigorous anti-utilitarian 'saw medical ethics as a code governing the duties of doctors ... [which are] derived from an anterior body of moral laws guaranteed by Christian philosophy'.

Undoubtedly the views of Enlightenment thinkers and their successors have freed the human spirit from the circumscribed boundaries then perceived by the Christian Church. Like a newly released bird ideas could fly in any direction they chose. Some philosophers chose to reject Christianity. Among these was the philosopher Hume who consciously rejected his Christian upbringing and all things Scottish in favour of the English values of the Union and its philosophy based on property.[33] Hume was such a sceptic that only a personal encounter with the living God would have shaken his personal agnosticism.[34] Although the views of the philosophers chimed with an age of reason they did not immediately challenge the Christian consensus. Thomas Percival, a Manchester physician who wrote his *Medical Ethics*[35] at the end of the eighteenth century to help doctors formalise their relationships in the rapidly expanding hospitals, was firmly committed to a belief in God although he was a disciple of the Arian heresy.[36] He rejected abortion except to protect the health of the mother; opposed duelling; defended human rights; and opposed assisted death. He advocated openness with patients on a scale which would make even the modern doctor hesitate.

Nevertheless slowly but insidiously the climate was changing. Medicine was now seen as a relentless battle with disease in which each scientific advance represented a new victory won. The new philosophies gradually seeped into the fabric of Medicine over more than a century to create a climate in which the central precepts of Christian belief and Hippocratic practice could be openly questioned by atheist philosophers in the twentieth century. It is difficult to identify precisely when the changing attitudes took place. Like so many cultural processes it was long drawn out. Ferguson[37] identifies the publication of Darwin's *Origin of the Species*. Undoubtedly the response of the Christian Church and its lamentable biblical exegesis created a watershed. Darwin himself doubted whether his evolutionary theory applied in the transition from primates to man and modern biblical exegesis reveals the self same ambiguity in the scriptures in its otherwise not inconsistent account of the same events. Students of ethics will no doubt wish to date the watershed at the publication in 1861 of the essay *Utilitarianism* by John Stuart Mill[38] which was much influenced by the philosophical views of Jeremy Bentham.

It seems not unreasonable two hundred years after the Enlightenment to enquire what new contribution to the sum of human happiness or understanding these new philosophies have made compared with Christian belief. I can detect little evidence either in Medicine or in society as a whole that any of the agnostic philosophies or any of the new political, economic or social theories is leading us inexorably forward to some as yet unachieved goal. Paul Johnson[39] assessed the lives of twelve intellectuals against the philosophies they themselves had espoused. His conclusions do not make encouraging reading. Most lacked any internal consistency and they consistently exempted themselves from the behaviour they demanded of others.

Alasdair McIntyre[40] is equally scathing. He writes in his study of moral theory *After Virtue* 'My own conclusion is very clear. It is that on the one hand we still, in spite of the efforts of three centuries of moral philosophy and one of sociology, lack any coherent, rationally defensible statement of a liberal individualistic point of view; and that on the other hand, the Aristotelian tradition can be restated in a way that restores intelligibility and rationality to our moral and social attitudes and commitment'. It was Aristotle who developed the concept of 'virtue' from earlier Socratic concepts. This was to be pursued for its own sake since virtue is more desirable than vice.[41] It offered a desirable objective – something for which we should strive. Aristotle accepted a supreme God from whom the desire to be virtuous emanates,[42] although he lived before the Christian dispensation. Christians would point to human frailty and original sin. They would look to the reconciling power of Jesus Christ and the power of the Holy Spirit to promote the pursuit of the virtue that we seek within us. Virtues include courage, both physical and moral.

For the doctor physical courage is manifest, like the plague doctors, in treating infectious disease patients at some personal risk to oneself. The refusal of some surgeons to treat HIV infected patients demonstrates a lack of virtue. Moral courage is seen in saying 'no' to patients when what they seek is not in their best interests or not a sensible use of health care resources. I have lost count of the number of times a doctor has written to me during my career saying, in effect, 'I know this treatment cannot be justified but the patient wants it and my duty is to the patient.' So *I* must show my moral courage, because the patient's doctor has failed to do so.

Significantly, Aristotle's 'virtue ethics' were developed by two saints of the Christian church – Augustine and Thomas Aquinas. These three provide for me the only sensible distillation upon which a coherent framework of medical ethics can be built.

Utilitarianism and what is sometimes called 'enlighten-ment thinking' dominated the medical ethics landscape but they offer no coherent framework for the complex clinical decisions doctors have to take.[43] Neither do they appeal to those noble ideals in mankind to which scripture regularly encourages Christians to aspire. Lord Hailsham of Marylebone[44] in his delightful little book *Values, Collapse and Cure*, beautiful not only for the thoughts it expresses but for the handwriting in which it is produced, says of Utilitarianism 'The greatest happiness of the greatest number denies that justice may ever assert the rights of a dissentient minority, or even a dissentient individual, against a powerful or intolerant majority or an unpopular against a popular opinion'.

McIntyre[45] is even more depressing. He concludes 'Moral philosophy, as it is dominantly understood, reflects the debates and disagreements of the culture so faithfully that its controversies turn out to be unsettlable in just the way that the political and moral debates are … it follows that our society cannot hope to achieve moral concensus.' Jeffrey Stout[46] is more optimistic. He believes that Western liber-alism is itself becoming one of the ethical traditions. He argues that while we each speak a language peculiar to our social role we are nevertheless all saying the same thing. Philosophical theories properly construed, he concludes, 'are not likely to endanger the moral inheritance of Western civilisation'! Nevertheless Stout himself believes that our major problem is 'the uneasy relation between social practices and such institutions as the capitalist market place and large scale bureaucracies'. Surely this is the very problem that we face in health care at this time both in the United Kingdom and the United States.

Historically Medicine has been concerned with the protection of its own status and privilege. Today there is little evidence of the pursuit of any wider noble ideal. The General Medical Council was set up, allegedly to protect the interests of patients. Stacey[47] reports that it bears striking resemblance to an exclusive gentleman's club more concerned with the protection of the profession's power and status. Certainly her remarkably gentle requests for change have been greeted with horror and hostility by the Council's hierarchy. Within the wider profession the not uniquely Christian concept of service to the patient is often challenged.

Experimental medicine seems intent upon the pursuit of knowledge without thought to the wider social implications that would result from application of the discovery. Does it matter if our healers become our executioners if society is thereby relieved of the economic burden of those who have outlived their usefulness? Lord Hailsham believes that it does. 'There is a congruence between the wise of all nations, cultures and languages as to the way in which all human beings ought to behave' Another great twentieth-century saint (I use the term in the Baptist sense) and Christian apologist, C. S. Lewis, described this congruence as 'the Tao'. Hailsham prefers 'natural morality' and, as a lawyer, sees a possible role for law. He goes on ... 'the primary thesis which I am seeking to support is that much of the troubles of the present world ... stem from a rejection of the conviction that these value judgments have a real meaning and an objective validity'. He adds, 'What is really wrong with society in this country and perhaps elsewhere is that we have lost our sense of values and the judgments and standards which embody and apply them ... a common factor which unites all value judgments in the ethical field is a sense of responsibility to something external to ourselves.'[48]

In Medicine, as in society as a whole, there *are* values which are enduring and which most human beings can recognise and applaud.

Yet surely this idea of something external to ourselves is not scientific. Is it not a hangover from a traditional myth long since discarded by scientific discovery? A case of an old man up there and 'pie in the sky when we die'? Such a concept of science is itself a myth. Time was when science seemed to offer certainty and the identification of inalienable laws.

Medicine seemed to produce the odd exception to such 'laws' but it was, after all, only an applied science and the exception could probably be explained by 'biological variation'. Moreover Medicine has always been a complex mixture of art and science. Galen believed that a doctor should be trained in both medicine and philosophy.[49] Perhaps our present preoccupation with science has made us neglect the philosophy which would help us clarify our 'core values'.[50]

Twentieth-century science has discovered uncertainty. Now we have relativity and quantum theory. Scientists cannot be relied upon to deal solely in objective facts. They, too, have their subjective theories. Einstein disapproved of quantum theory. Eddington ridiculed the idea of black holes and probably delayed their discovery by thirty years.[51] Kitty Ferguson in her book *The Fire in the Equations* finds that ' ... the assumptions which underlie science are as unprovable and logically indefensible as those which underlie religion

Christian Values in Medicine

– in fact they are largely the same assumptions'.[52] Although science and religion adopt fundamentally different methods, there is surprising agreement in overall approach. Both seek to systematise observations and draw out principles and both allow that exceptions to such rules will occur. Indeed if they did not, science would never advance. Leonard Bernstein in the opening solo of his Mass wrote 'Sing God a simple song for God is the simplest of all.' In her inimical American way Kitty Ferguson comments 'Find a word for God which implies ultimate truth without insisting on the notion of a person and many an agnostic scientist will sing along with Bernstein.'[53] Philosophy may not yet be ready for a similar capitulation but an increasing number of its leading figures find Christian belief and values more satisfying intellectually than any of the alternatives.

These broad sweeps of science and philosophy may seem to have remarkably little direct relevance for Medicine and its ethics. Indeed consideration of moral problems and ethical dilemmas has occupied little more than the last twenty years of the BMA ethics committee's ninety-three-year-old existence. In the year in which Westminster Cathedral was founded, the BMA's annual meeting included an ethical section for the first time. Its considerations included: control over irregular practice; unqualified assistants; professional etiquette; advertising; employment issues; medical defence and medical status.

The first three decades of the committee's work were spent adjudicating disputes between doctors. Then in 1937 the first real modern ethical dilemma emerged when the Matrimonial Causes Act required doctors to take sides in a divorce when one party was mentally ill. After an interruption by the Second World War the Association became involved in measures to prevent a repeat of the horrific Nazi medical experiments[54] in Germany. It is not often appreciated how much German doctors were implicated in the rise of National

Socialism,[55] a situation for which current German doctors have done much to atone. This was followed by a further lull in the historical development of medical ethics.

Finally at the beginning of the 1970s moral problems began, at last, to assert the dominant role they have today when they now account for more than three-quarters of the issues discussed and almost the whole of the available debating time. Nevertheless the contrasts are striking. The Working Party on Euthanasia set up (curiously) by the Board of Education and Science and which published its report in January 1971,[56] carefully dissected and opposed all the arguments that had been expressed for the practice of medically assisted death in the previous decade of 'the Swinging Sixties'. In contrast, the working party established in 1986 undertook a thorough review of both sides of the argument, considered apparently similar situations of justifiable homicide, and the chairman and selected secretariat visited the Netherlands.[57] While its conclusions are reported to have disappointed its humanist secretary[58] the Association was no longer prejudging the issues.

The abortion debate had occurred during this quiescent period when the Central Ethical Committee appeared to be asleep or, more correctly, preoccupied with other matters. Indeed the profession seemed almost taken by surprise by the change in the law. There is little evidence in the historical record to suggest that the issues were ever seriously debated at the Annual Representative Meeting and certainly not by the usual method of a specialist working party.

Conversely the historical record does show a rather sordid and shabby 'political' response to the question of artificial fertility. Cameron[59] notes that 'a prominent British gynaecologist' vigorously argued in favour of allowing the research to continue as recommended by the Warnock Committee[60] of which he was a member and active apologist. This same senior gynaecologist was equally involved in the debates on the matter within the BMA. Indeed, the chairman of the Central Ethical Committee is quoted as being 'reassured' by his advice. In retrospect, some of the information seems less clear cut. Nevertheless utilitarianism won the day. Perhaps this should not surprise us. As Payne remarks the 'flow' in modern medical ethics is towards the greatest good for the greatest number. 'Since pleasure is the goal of utility, medicine is inclined to be another servant of a hedonistic society'.[61] Yet as Doherty reminds us 'its deficiencies become apparent when practical decisions are taken. It is based on a cost benefit analysis of consequences and treats human values as quantitatively comparable items . . .'[62]

Does this process have to continue its relentless progression? Is there no possibility, as Payne implies, that individual moral considerations can be promoted in Medicine? Has the tradition of virtue ethics no place in the consideration of moral dilemmas within modern medicine? Has a Christian ethic nothing to offer to debates about the sanctity of life whether of the foetus or of the elderly demented person? Is Christianity destined to be marginalised in these crucial debates? I believe that it is absolutely essential that the contribution which Christian faith can make must not merely be added to the ethical agenda but must begin to dominate that agenda.

The residue of Christian faith among doctors remains strong and provides fertile soil for the re-creation of a distinctively Judaeo-Christian ethic within Medicine. I sense a much greater proportion of Christian believers in the health care professions than in the population at large. Such an entirely empirical observation fits well with what we would theoretically expect. As Jack Aitken and his colleagues reminded us in 1984, the practice of Medicine is, after the ordained ministry, pre-eminently in keeping with the spirit and practice of the Christian faith.[63] This must surely have been one of the chief underlying factors which has encouraged so many Christians down the centuries to offer their services to humanity in the ranks of Medicine and Nursing. The historical record is impressive. The Christian Church has played a major – some would even argue a decisive – role in the development of Western civilisation. Some months ago an *Independent* leader writer, commenting on the dismissal of an Anglican cleric for his declared unbelief in God, claimed that all great civilisations required a belief – and the implication was a religious belief – in something if they were to survive and prosper.

Christians have made enormous financial contributions to Medicine. It was the Church which made possible large numbers of 'hospices' and 'hospitals' as their conspicuous absence in parts of the world dominated by other philosophies readily attests. As Christian missions have moved out into other lands and continents, medical missions have followed closely behind. The Hospital Sunday Fund founded in 1873 involved an annual church collection from which, initially, provincial hospitals benefited even more than the London Voluntary Hospitals who had primarily hoped to gain.[64] 'In those periods when the spiritual health of the church has been at its best, its practical influence in the medical world has been correspondingly evident'.[65]

Few Christians would dare to claim that the spiritual health of the Western Church is 'at its best' today. Nevertheless, as Elijah was gently reminded, there remains an effective remnant in Medicine upon which a revival of distinctly Christian values can be built. It is, however, essential that both doctors and theologians embrace new knowledge and modern philosophical debate rather than adopting positions that appear to be easy to defend. The pronouncements of some Christian theologians on modern ethical problems in Medicine have been embarrassing in their naïvety.

One does not have to believe that life begins at conception to hold the foetus to be a precious member of the human race fashioned in the image of God.[66] It is logically defensible and philosophically sound[67] to believe that it is wrong to kill patients but permissible not to impose life-prolonging treatment against their express wishes. The road back from Society's present ethical dead end will be a long and arduous one. We shall only be partially retracing our steps. At some point we shall rejoin the road which leads to the promised celestial city. Christians do not believe that this universe continues indefinitely. As scripture teaches, and an increasing number of scientists believe, it had an unambiguous beginning. Scripture tells us that it has a finite end. We are not to waste our time in endless speculation but to get on redeeming a fallen world until the Lord gives us a greater task to do in His new heaven and new earth.

A small obscure group of doctors in ancient Greece captured the hearts and minds of their professional colleagues and established principles which have proved to be of enduring quality for more than two thousand years. Can Christian doctors in the United Kingdom on the threshold of the twenty-first century not recapture those values in a society which has tasted the nostrums peddled by ethical quacks and found that they simply do not work? No more fitting gift could be made to the many silent witnesses to the Christian faith of our predecessors in times infinitely more hostile to Christian belief than our own.

Notes
1 British Medical Association (and others), *Core Values for the Medical Profession*, report of a conference, 3/4 November 1994, London, BMA.
2 British Medical Association (1995), Annual Representative Meeting (Harrogate), minute 202.

3 British Medical Association (1988), *Philosophy and Practice of Medical Ethics*, London, BMA.

4 British Medical Association (1993), *Medical Ethics Today – Its Practice & Philosophy*, London, BMA.

5 Francis, H. (1985), review article 'In the Service of Medicine', *The Journal of the Christian Medical Fellowship*, 31.1, pp. 25–7, London, CMF, Waterloo Road.

6 Keown, J. (1994), book review in *Light and Salt*, 6.1, pp. 14–15, April 1994, London, CARE, 53 Romney Street.

7 Saunders, M. (1994), book review in *British Medical Journal*, 308, pp. 885–90.

8 Cameron, Nigel M. De S (1991), *The New Medicine: Life and Death after Hippocrates*, Wheaton, Illinois, Crossway Books.

9 Pappworth, M. H. (1967), *Human Guinea Pigs – experimentation on man*, London, Routledge & Kegan Paul.

10 Lock, S. & Wells, F. (1993), *Fraud & Misconduct in Medical Research*, London, BMJ publishing group.

11 St Matthew 16: 18 (Douai Bible; NIV).

12 Kosserev, I. and Crawshaw, R. (1994), 'Medicine and the Gulag', *British Medical Journal*, 304, pp. 1726–30.

13 Richards, D. W. (1973), 'Hippocrates and History: The Arrogance of Humanism', p. 23 in *Hippocrates revisited – a search for meaning*, Bulger, R. J., ed., New York, Medcom Press.

14 Jonsen, A. R. (1990), *The New Medicine and the old ethics*, Cambridge, Massachusetts and London, England, Harvard University Press, p. 171.

15 Carrick, P. (1985), *Medical Ethics in Antiquity*, Dordrecht, Holland, D. Reidel publishing company.

16 Temkin, O. (1991) *Hippocrates in a World of Pagans and Christians*, Baltimore and London, John Hopkins University Press.

17 MacKinney, L. C. (1952), 'Medical Ethics and Etiquette in the early middle ages: The persistence of

Hippocratic ideals', *Bulletin of the History of Medicine*, 26, pp. 1–31.

18 Temkin, op. cit., p. 241.

19 MacKinney, op. cit.

20 Kibre, P. (1945) 'Hippocratic Writings in the Middle Ages', *Bulletin of the History of Medicine*, 18, pp. 371–412.

21 Aitken, J. T., Fuller, H. W. C. and Johnson, D. (1984), *The Influence of Christians in Medicine*, London, CMF.

22 Cunningham, A. (1989), *Thomas Sydenham: epidemics, experiment and the 'Good Old Cause'* in *The Medical Revolution of the seventeenth century*, French, R. and Wear, A., eds, Cambridge University Press.

23 Kass, A. M. and Kass, E. H. (1988), *Perfecting the World: The life and times of Dr Thomas Hodgkin 1798–1866*, Boston, Harcourt, Brace & Jovanovich.

24 Grell, O. P. (1933), 'Conflicting duties: Plague and the obligations of early modern physicians towards patients & Commonwealth in England & the Netherlands' in *Doctors & Ethics: The earlier historical setting of professional ethics*, Amsterdam, Atlanta G. A. Rodopi.

25 Aitken, op. cit., p. 70.

26 Fissell, M. E. (1993), 'Innocent and honourable bribes' in *The codification of medical morality*, Baker, R., Porter, D. and Porter, R., eds, Dordrecht/Boston/London, Kluwer Academic Publishers.

27 Porter, R. (1993), 'Plutus or Hygiea – Thomas Beddoes and the crisis of medical ethics at the turn of the nineteenth century' in *The codification of medical morality*, Baker, R., Porter, D. and Porter R., eds, Dordrecht/Boston/London, Kluwer Academic Publishers.

28 Clouse, R. G., Pierard, R. V., Yamauchi, E. M. (1993), *Two Kingdoms: The church and culture through the ages*, Chicago, Moody Press, p. 374.

29 Smith, A. (1776), *The Wealth of Nations*, Penguin Classics 1986, Harmondsworth, Penguin Books.

30 Suzuki, A. (1995), 'Anti-Lockean Enlightenment? Mind and Body in Early Eighteenth Century English Medicine' in *Medicine in the Enlightenment*, Porter, R., ed, Amsterdam, Atlanta G. A. Rodopi.

31 French, R. (1993), 'Ethics in the eighteenth century: Hoffman in Halle' in *Doctors and Ethics: the earlier historical setting of professional ethics*, Amsterdam, Atlanta G. A. Rodopi.

32 Porter, R. (1993), 'Thomas Gisborne: Physicians, Christians and Gentlemen' in *Doctors and Ethics: The earlier historical setting of professional ethics*, Amsterdam, Atlanta G. A. Rodopi.

33 McIntyre, A. (1988), *Whose justice? Which rationality,* Notre Dame, Indiana, University of Notre Dame Press.

34 Ferguson, K. (1994), *The Fire in the Equations*, London, Bantam Press.

35 Percival, T. (1803), *Medical Ethics; or a code of institutes and precepts adapted to the professional conduct of physicians and surgeons*, London, J. Johnson.

36 Percival, E. (1807), *Memoirs of the life and writings of Thomas Percival M.D.*, London, J. Johnson.

37 Ferguson, op. cit.

38 Mill, J. S. (1861), *Utilitarianism*, Penguin Classics (1987), Harmondsworth, Penguin Books.

39 Johnson, P. (1989), *Intellectuals*, London, George Weidenfeld & Nicholson Ltd.

40 McIntyre, A. (1985), *After Virtue – a study in moral theory*, London, Gerald Duckworth and Co. Ltd.

41 Lloyd, G. E. R. (1978), *Hippocratic Writings*, Penguin Classics, Harmondsworth, Penguin Books, p. 259.

42 Lloyd, G. E. R. (1968), *Aristotle: The growth and structure of his thought*, CUP.

43 Maclean, A. (1993), *The elimination of morality – Reflections on Utilitarianism and Bioethics*, London and New York, Routledge.

44 Lord Hailsham of Marylebone (1994) *Values, Collapse and Cure*, London, Harper Collins, p. 85.
45 McIntyre, op. cit., p. 252.
46 Stout, J. (1988), *Ethics after Babel: The languages of morals and their discontents*, Cambridge, James Clarke & Co. pp. 265, 288.
47 Stacey, M. (1992), *Regulating British Medicine – The General Medical Council*, Chichester, John Wiley.
48 Hailsham, op. cit., pp. 91, 132, 148–9.
49 Temkin, op. cit., p. 49.
50 BMA, *Core Values*, op. cit.
51 Ferguson, op. cit., p. 67, pp. 66–7.
52 Ferguson, op. cit., p. 270.
53 Ferguson, op. cit., p. 62
54 Berger, R.L. (1990), 'Nazi Science – The Dachau hypothermia experiments', *New England Journal of Medicine*, 322, pp. 1435–40.
55 Hanauske-Abel, H. M. (1986), 'From nazi holocaust to nuclear holocaust; A lesson to learn', *The Lancet*, 328, p. 272.
56 British Medical Association (1971), *The problem of euthanasia*, a report by a special panel appointed by the Board of Science & Education, London, BMA.
57 British Medical Association (1988), *Euthanasia*, Report of a Working Party, London, BMA.
58 Taylor, P. (1991), 'Profiles in Responsibility', John Dawson, *The PSR Quarterly*, 1, pp. 165–8.
59 Cameron, op. cit.
60 Department of Health and Social Security (1984), *Report of the Committee of Inquiry into Human Fertilisation and Embryology*, Cmnd 9314, London, HMSO, p. 110.
61 Payne, F.E. (1985), *The Christian and the practice of Medicine*, Milford, Michigan, USA, Mott Media Inc.
62 Doherty, P. (1983), *Medical Ethics*, Westbury-on-Trym, Bristol, Guild of Catholic Doctors.

63 Aitken, op. cit., p. 1.
64 Rivett, G. (1986), *The development of the London Hospital System 1823–1982*, London, King Edward's Hospital Fund for London, p. 121.
65 Aitken, op. cit., p. 2.
66 Berry, C. (1993), *Beginnings: Christian views of the Early Embryo*, London, CMF, p. 40.
67 Maclean, op. cit., p. 39.

John Tavener

Leading Composer

John Tavener was born in 1944 and educated at Highgate School. At the Royal Academy of Music he won several major prizes for composition and in 1968 his dramatic cantata *The Whale*, given in the debut concert of the London Sinfonietta, took its audience by storm.

Over the years the contemplative side of his nature has led him in more spiritual directions and his commitment to the Russian Orthodox Church, which he joined in 1977, is now evident in all his work. Recent major pieces include a setting of the complete *Orthodox Vigil Service*; *The Akathist of Thanksgiving*; *The Protecting Veil* for solo cello and strings; large-scale choral and orchestral works, *Resurrection*, *We Shall See Him As He Is* and *The Apocalypse*; and an opera *Mary of Egypt*.

Premieres in 1995 included *Let's Being Again*, for chorus, instruments and children; *Svyatuiee* for Steven Isserlis and the Kiev Chamber Choir; *Innocence*, written to commemorate the victims of World War II and *Agraphon*, commissioned to form the centre piece of a Tavener festival in Athens.

A major BBC Festival was recently devoted to his music and *Glimpses of Paradise*, a documentary on Tavener, was screened for the first time on BBC Television in 1992.

John Tavener's music is performed internationally and is widely available under various labels.

John Tavener
Christian Values in Music

Art and the End-point – *in memory of Philip Sherrard*

If we are to rediscover the primordial ideas of a religious or metaphysical tradition in art and life, then we must turn to the masters of this tradition. The magnificent scope of the *logos* doctrine with its cosmic dimension – the idea of God incarnate in all human and created existence, largely abandoned by Western Christendom, has to be reinstated. It is only with the profoundest humility of the Early Saints of the Desert that we can even begin this almost impossible task. As a composer living at the end of the twentieth century, I am forever daunted by this work, fighting innovation and modernism in all their hideous manifestations ... to rediscover the transparent, and the numinous, and crawling on all fours, forever to begin again, and again, and again.

7

My subject is the sacred in art – art that is *athanatos*, without death, without change, without beginning and without end.

This is well-nigh impossible to discuss in a time when Man has lost his belief not only in God, but also in himself. Do we live in a culture in ruins, as Father Symeon from Mount Athos has suggested?

Without doubt, the modern concept of the artist as creative genius would probably have excluded him from Plato's Greece, because any artist who produced a work of sacred art could never think of himself as a creative genius in the modern sense of the word. The artist of the sacred con-creates, reproduces, must submit to the discipline of practising, through endless repetition of a given form, until he has mastered all of it, so that its original transcendence begins to flow through him; no longer a matter of external copying or repetition, but a matter of directing the forces of primordial inspiration, of which he is now the vehicle, into formal patterns that long practice and meditation have allowed him to master both inwardly and outwardly. I would say that the dictum for all sacred Christian art must be as St Paul expresses it in another context: 'It is not I that live, but Christ in me': or as the great Islamic poet and saint, Rumi, put it, 'I am a dead man walking.'

As a composer, living and working in these secular times, I work in an area which seems to concern more and more people. My increasing concern for the sacred needs some explanation. For an artist to work in a sacred tradition, he must first believe in the Divine Realities that inform that particular tradition. This is a *sine qua non* – not of course a guarantee for great art – but it is an indispensable requirement. Second, he must know the traditions of his art. He must know the tools, so that he can work with material that is primordial, and therefore not 'his'; not his or her expression, but the tradition working through him.

The artist concerned with the sacred must make an act of faith. In my own case, it was a commitment to the Orthodox Church. First and foremost a commitment to Christ-God as expressed through the eyes of the Orthodox Church. This is radical in the purest sense of the word and demands a gradual losing of self through a work of endless repentance, constantly falling, but picking oneself up, pointing evermore God-wards, to provide the vehicle through which the only Creator can work.

There is nothing 'pie in the sky' about this; the task is daunting, awesome and exigent, and at the end of the day one can expect nothing but crucifixion and failure, because our strength, unique as Christians, lies in our weakness, our frailty and our vulnerability. And, perhaps most of all, the task is daunting, because I am a Western composer writing within the ethos and framework of the Eastern Orthodox Church. It has always seemed to me that in the Greek East, man starts with God: God around him, God in everything that he sees, and that in the Latin West, man begins with 'man', and then aspires towards God. This is reflected in the vastly different theology, the vastly different approaches, the vastly different emphases, and the vastly different art, architecture and music.

So you can see not only is the task daunting spiritually, but it is daunting in specific musical terms. Because if an English composer wishes to write music within the Orthodox tradition, he must, like an icon painter, renounce any ideas of his own, and adhere to a strict discipline based on a system of tones – tone 1, tone 2, tone 3, tone 4, tone 5, tone 6, tone 7 and tone 8. Each tone is different, somewhat like Indian ragas, somewhat like the Gregorian modes, but unlike these insofar as every Orthodox country has developed its own tone system. For instance, there are eight Greek tones, eight Russian tones, eight Coptic tones and so on. All these tones have probably evolved from the dawn of civilisation (probably well over one hundred of them). Indeed one can see many connections between the Greek tones and the Indian ragas.

It would take a lifetime to become fully acquainted with even one of these tone systems. If in Byzantine times a melodist was asked to set anything to music, he would first have to set it in the appropriate tone or melody. The music is as much part of the tapestry and strict discipline of the Church as is the iconography. If for instance a composer was asked to set a text to the Mother of God, he would first have to know on which feast day this was proposed, because all eight tones may be needed for one single text, depending on whether the text is to be sung in Lent, Easter, Pentecost or any other day in the Church's year.

I often wonder why the sacred music of any age should sound very different. The answer is that it shouldn't. If composers in the West concerned with sacred tradition were trained in the disciplines of Byzantium, sacred India, music of the Sufis, Judaic chant or any of the Orthodoxies, instead of learning about Schoenberg's innovations they would become aware that innovation has nothing to do with tradition. That is why no innovatory art can possess the magisterial, primordial beauty emanating from the divine, making us creatures through which a theophany could pass.

People talk about composers finding their own voice; this is another totally misleading concept. Not misleading if the composer does not believe in Divine Realties; then of course he can be totally promiscuous in his artistic pursuits, and there is nothing wrong with this. It only becomes wrong if he believes in Divine Realities and, at the same time, digs from the endless so-called innovations from the last four hundred years. I speak of the scientific revolution of the sixteenth, seventeenth and eighteenth centuries, which brought about in Western art and religion the dominant world-view of modern times, indeed a progressive degeneration that characterises every sphere of our contemporary life.

You can perhaps begin to see why the Orthodox find the concept of an anthem or a hymn totally incomprehensible. To us it holds up proceedings, and instead of encouraging prayer and contemplation, it seems to introduce the idea of an entertainment or a concert into the middle of a sacred ceremony. No wonder Stravinsky referred to Mozart's Masses as 'operatic sweets of sin'.

The icon is a supreme example of Christian art and of transcendence and transfiguration. It possesses simplicity, transfigured beauty and austerity. Austerity because the manner of painting has remained unchanged since the first mandelion (or 'icon not painted by human hands') bearing the face of Christ miraculously imprinted on a piece of material and sent to the King of Edessa. Icon painting is a strict discipline, requiring fasting and constant communion. An icon does not express emotion (it is geometric and its colour palette is severely limited) and yet to the believer it inspires awe, wonder and the reverence of kissing. The icon is in one sense beyond art because it plunges us straight into liturgical time and sacred history. But what makes a great icon? I believe that it is the Holy Spirit working through the painter, and that is a total mystery.

How far can the art of icon painting relate to music? I will suggest some ways on which the composer may meditate. If the composer knows something of the sacred tones of the Orthodox Church he will have the material. If he understands the significance of the 'ison' or drone, then he will have some clues. The composer may dance out of or back into the tone, but it must always be somewhere present. He must also limit the tonal and colour palette, but always knowing where he must insert the Divine archetype by a fully assimilated knowledge of the tones. In other words, the one is the other, the archetype is the icon, the icon is the archetype, there is an indissoluble interpenetration of the one by the other. The numinous presence, of which the outward form of things is the image, is also present within it. Though there is a distinction there is no dualism between the natural and the supernatural world. Hence, the same must apply to music.

Why this set of intervals? What is its divine archetype? Why this series of chords? What is its divine archetype? Why this rhythm? – so that the music can be analysed in a specifically metaphysical way, and also listened to in a specifically metaphysical manner. Unfortunately the spiritually impoverished state of music criticism finds itself unable to do this, because in order to understand these concepts, it is necessary to understand a kind of knowledge that has nothing to do with reason. Blessed Augustine defined it as 'Wisdom uncreate'. And in order to understand 'Wisdom uncreate' contemporary life must cease to be stifled by a cult of experimentation, art for art's sake, and a kind of specialisation that characterises every form of mental activity, requiring only a tiny fraction of our intelligence. This is the condemnation, and until the concept of 'Wisdom uncreate' is reunderstood, our civilisation will continue to commit mass suicide with all the relentlessness of a Greek tragedy.

The Church is no longer the wise patron that she was in the Byzantine period, the Medieval Western period, or in Bach's Protestant Germany. As artists, we literally write or paint into a vacuum and into an apparent spiritual void. The point of any sacred art, however, is that it should be functional. Think of Egyptian wall paintings, Muslim architecture, Bach passions, Byzantine icons, the Cathedral of Saint Sophia, the Taj Mahal – all once functional and now in danger of becoming museums: out of the Church, into the concert hall, out of the Church, into the art gallery, out of the Temple, into the greedy anonymous hands of dealers, along with the terrifying devastation of God's world.

This is all part of the desecration of the sacred. Surely all creation, in all its fullness, is the necessary expression of Divine Life, with all the absolute freedom and spontaneity of God's being. Otherwise we face the appalling idea of the conception of a creation created outside God, deprived of His immanent presence, and with no living roots in Him, and thus ultimately of a purely materialistic character only. It is not accident, because of what I have said about the Western scientific revolution, that a purely materialistic view of the physical world arose first of all in the *Western* Christian world, not in the Orthodox East, not in the Celtic tradition, not in the Hindu, Buddhist traditions and not in the Islamic world.

My setting of a hymn to the Mother of God from the divine liturgy of St Basil the Great speaks of her cosmic power and beauty over a shattered world – *'all* creation rejoices'. The idea of the cosmological role of the Mother of God does of course depend on things which I regard as fundamental to the whole spirit of Orthodoxy. This is what might be called its symbolic or iconic realism. But without her 'Yes' at the Annunciation there would be no Christ, no salvation and no Life.

I see the act of recreating in the end as a miracle. After the ascetic pain of labouring to find the best way that I can to depict the subject, then this miracle happens. But also each new piece is an act of repentance, stripping away unessentials, ever more naked, ever more simple ... one might even say ever more foolish. One tries in one's work to follow the life of the Saint, even if it appears completely unobtainable. Through ascetic struggle the Saint reintegrates himself into the paradisial life. Again and again his or her life is associated with a variety of forms of reconciliation to nature, to trees, to plants, to climate: the enduring of heat and cold, the eating with no ill effects of noxious weeds, friendship with wild animals. This is the traditional view of the Saint, common to all great Orthodoxies. One of the greatest saints and poets of the patristic age was St Ephrem the Syrian. The imagery of his poetry rivals, if not surpasses that of Dante. 'Thunder entered her' is a wonderful example of symbolic and iconic realism.

Now comes a more practical problem. How does one communicate to a world that has forgotten and has little time for repentance, simplicity or foolishness? – the foolishness of Christ-God, the foolishness of the Mother of God and the foolishness of all the crowds of martyrs, Saints and holy fools. I said, however, that the world had forgotten, and this seems to me to be the operative word, otherwise why has there been a resurgence of sacred art towards the close of the millennium. Think of Pappadiamandis, think of Yeats, think of late Stravinsky, Messiaen, T. S. Eliot, St Jean Perse, think of Seferis, the late poetry of Sikelianos, think of David Jones, Eric Gill, Cecil Collins, think of Arvo Pärt, and I suppose myself – but also think of this century's great traditional metaphysicians – Guénon, Corbin, Coomaraswamy, Marco Pallis, Philip Sherrard and a whole host of others. *Eonia* is a piece which came to me already fully grown. It is a short piece which sprang from the death of a beloved friend, Cecil Collins, who spent his life devoted to the sacred, painting fools and angels. He was always outside any religious tradition, but he used the world of archetypes that he considered to be more universal. He would take from the Sufi tradition, the early Christian tradition, the

Hindu tradition, and indeed any sacred tradition that he felt to be relevant to his art. I think of *Eonia* as an essence, a fragrance, a Haiku, but above all a tribute to the man I loved and whose frail iconographical art touched me deeply.

Another piece was inspired by the death of a friend. Athene was a young, talented Greek actress who was tragically killed in a cycling accident. The music came to me at her funeral. It seemed to be her parting gift to me.

We are witnessing a profound amnesia of simple, primordial and eternal truths, in favour of an insane, technological, materialistic, psychological, intellectual culture. A culture and spirituality in ruins. Devoid of *gnosis*, as T. S. Eliot predicted, a civilisation that rejects what it cannot diminish. If, as I say, the operative word is 'forgotten' then there must be a ray of hope. To reawaken the primordial consciousness that lies dormant in all of us, somehow we have to provide a *temenos* or sacred space in which to work.

The concert hall, the opera house and the art gallery are all glaring reminders of how fragmented and dislocated we have become. Stockhausen has said the churches will become the concert halls of the future, and there is more than a ring of truth about this. To move the *temenos* back into the cathedrals and churches, not to popularise and desanctify even more, but to allow sacred art to breathe gently on the ancient stones. Let the great medieval cathedrals of England be used to breathe back anew the medieval thought or *gnosis* that formed them, because it is only through the world of imagination, or through the intellective and visionary organ that lies dormant in most of us, that we can live in an Eternal Now – the home and beginning of all life and of all becoming.

And if the Christian Church is to offer a positive response to the challenge of the sacred and to the ecological crisis, it must understand the colossal significance and implication of the Incarnation, in all its amplitude and magnificence.

As the Orthodox Christmas service of Compline proclaims, 'God is *with* us, understand ye nations, God is *with* us.'

Adherence to primordial tradition requires a very deep humility; a humility that at the end of the day says, in the Platonic sense, we know nothing; a humility that requires a complete dismantling of the whole present scientific, psychological, popularist, profane and radical dehumanisation of our society, and a comprehension of God that is so deep in its non-literal understanding and humility, that we can only pray with the Fathers of the Church in tiny sentences ... 'Help me' or ... 'as You know and as You will, have mercy'. Theology in the Orthodox East has always been regarded as an expression of a given reality, but in the West, largely due to the disastrous teachings of Aristotle, instead of the Platonic elements which had served early Eastern theologians as a vehicle for expressing an understanding of man, confirmed through a life of prayer and contemplation, Western Aristotelian thought entered a ruinous epoch of abstraction and theory.

In the West, art has become abstracted and removed from its eucharistic function, removed also from nature, from its sacramental roots and finally removed from life itself. Is there anywhere in the world today where the right notes or tones have to be found before parliament can be opened? This show how far we have strayed, because it was the norm in Plato's Greece, so integrated were art, metaphysics and life. The closest I get to Plato's Greece is in being asked to write music for occasions of great significance. For instance, I was asked by Canterbury Cathedral to write an Acclamation for the Ecumenical Patriarch, His All Holiness Demetrios II on the historic occasion of his entering Canterbury Cathedral.

Another special occasion was the VE Day service at St Paul's Cathedral, in 1995, and for this I wrote three short antiphons.

I believe that we are in an abnormal state, this split

Christian Values

between imagination, reason, art and metaphysics. Our art is separated from sacred cosmology and the teachings of the Fathers on the anthropological aspects of the sacramental nature of creation. Out on a limb from the sacred, English hymns have references to God and the saints, but they have nothing to do with sacred art. A great deal of art expresses intimations of the divine, aspirations of the divine, glimpses of the divine, either in the human soul or in the world of nature. However, the quality that distinguishes a work of sacred art and that sets it apart from other works of art, is one that can only be described by a word such as 'knowledge' or *'gnosis'*. As Dante wrote:

> You who have sound intellects, seek out the doctrine that conceals itself beneath the veil of the strange verses ...

Indeed this invites all of us to seek out 'the intellect of love' – a disposition of being that induces and permits the God that constantly desires to reveal himself (if only we could see in our soul) and desires our power of vision. But never forget that the great twentieth-century Greek poet, Seferis, said towards the end of his life that it was not among the academic, artistic, or ecclesiastical world that he found 'the intellect of love', but in the illiterate country people of Greece, because they already possessed it, albeit subliminally. So unless we are all able to rediscover this 'intellect of love', or this 'Wisdom uncreate' (call it what you will) we will never find our way out of the spiritual, theological, ecological and artistic catastrophe that faces us at the close of the twentieth century.

I am neither philosopher nor theologian, but my work – my work of repentance that may or may not lead me towards a sacred art – can be judged only by how near the music I write comes to its task. This is my work within the vast area from which I must continue to dig and labour and to try to resituate the modern mentality as a whole within the framework of metaphysical values and wisdom from which it has been so disastrously uprooted.

I would like to end, however, on a more apophatic note, perhaps you might even say on a more apocalyptic note, at any rate on a question mark. How childlike, and how deep must be our trust in God in the face of the apocalyptic events that are happening around us day by day. How childlike and how immeasurably deep must have been the faith of the Mother of God when the Archangel appeared to her and she exclaimed, terror-struck, 'How shall this be?' No amount of writing, philosophising, poetry, music or painting can in the end give any absolute answer. Faith and doubt go hand in hand, and we love both the faith and the doubt equally. The Mother of God trusted, you might say madly, blindly, insanely, at the conception of God into her womb. We try hard and continue to follow her example of the joy of believing and yet not knowing, and the piercing agony of watching her Son crucified day after day, hour after hour, and forever asking her question, 'How shall this be?'

'Be humble and you will remain whole, be bent and you will remain straight ... Appear plainly and hold to simplicity.' Our artistic and Christian attitude must be what, for want of better words, I would call 'the poverty of innocence'. Today the world places a high value on sophistication, on being worldly wise, on being technically clever, or on being professional. Christianity and art of the end point place no value whatsoever on these qualities. Truly Christian art requires a total rejection of all of this. The first priority is that our heart must be soft and warm with the living, wounded and vulnerable spirit. If we do not have this warm heart, this living wounded life, we must ask God to give it, trying ourselves to do those things by which we can acquire it. Most of all, we have to see that we have *not* got it – that we *are* cold. The one thing, the only thing that can save us is simplicity. And this simplicity leads to the last revolution left to our dying civilisation – the Beatitudes of Christ. 'Let us become God for Him, who became man because of us.'

This means that if we are to see things as they are, we have to free ourselves completely from any kind of pseudo-knowledge and the methodologies that go with it. We have to free ourselves from all that we think we know, empty our own minds of all that we think we know, of all the conceptions we have formed as a result of going in pursuit of a knowledge we think we have obtained through our own efforts. For true knowledge cannot be acquired by any of these means. True knowledge has its source in the Wisdom or Sofía that is the life blood of all things and where everything is already known. The Mother of God is herself this Wisdom, this Sofía, and she points us, as she does in every icon, towards God. This does not mean that we are excused from the hell of modern life. On the contrary, we must plunge into the abyss, go through this hell, and accept it knowing it is the love of God that causes our suffering.

Here is a Christianity that is not only unsafe and uncomfortable, but it has all the untamed ferocity of the desert, and may demand martyrdom, suffering, and a path where we can 'get involved', where we can become on fire to serve God. 'As an unconquerable token of victory, an invincible shield and a divine sceptre, we worship thy most holy cross, O Christ, whereby the world has been saved and Adam filled with joy.' And then, only then can we begin to say with the Mother of God, however tentatively, 'How shall this be?' Having asked this question, our lives, our art and our work will already have begun to stumble on to the road towards the End Point, which ultimately leads to Christ crucified – Christ risen and alive for ever.

Rt Hon
Sir Edward Heath KG MBE MP

Former Prime Minister, Sailor and Musician

Sir Edward Heath was born in 1916 and educated at Chatham House School, Ramsgate and Balliol College, Oxford. He has been an MP continuously since 1950 and is currently Father of the House of Commons, the longest serving member.

During his time in Parliament he has held various appointments including Government Chief Whip, 1955; Minister of Labour, 1959; leader of the Conservative Party, 1965; Prime Minister, 1970–4. As Prime Minister he completed the negotiations in 1971 for Britain's entry into the European Economic Community in 1973. Since resigning from the leadership of the Conservative Party, Sir Edward has travelled extensively – to China and Japan many times and other Far Eastern countries, to North and South America and to most European countries. In 1990 he paid a special visit to Iraq to negotiate the release of more than a hundred British hostages held at the start of the Gulf War.

Outside politics, Sir Edward enjoys sailing and has found time to win trophies at international level. His other great love is music and he has conducted many orchestras both at home and abroad. He was Chairman of the London Symphony Orchestra Trust 1963–70 and has made a number of recordings.

In 1992 Sir Edward was appointed a Knight Companion of the Most Noble Order of the Garter.

Sir Edward Heath
Christian Values in Politics

Peace and Justice:
a View of the Past and a Vision for the Future

Sir Edward addresses the major issues of peace and justice within a national and international context. He outlines his vision for the future of Europe and the way in which closer co-operation between the major powers can help to reduce conflict and inequality both at home and abroad.

8

Reflecting on my life in politics, which is now just over forty-five years, I realised that the changes in the relationships between the ecclesiastical authorities in this country have really been quite remarkable and far greater than at any other time in our own history; and I think this has proved to be of the utmost importance to our country as well as to others of the Christian faith. It is also true to say that Westminster Cathedral has played a very important part in all this, as have all those people, from the Cardinal onwards, who have handled these affairs. So today we see, on many occasions, that the leaders of the different Churches in this country are all together and taking part not only in ceremonial but, rather more than that, also in the actual proceedings. When I watch them sometimes I smile slightly when I see the look on some of their faces as if they rather doubt whether they ought to be there. But I'm sure it's right that they should be and that this is of benefit to everyone concerned. We have made astonishing progress in our co-operation between those of all the Christian faiths shown in the Churches of our own country, and on this they are all to be commended.

It has also occurred to me that, in all my time in the House of Commons, no one in my constituency, and no one in any place I've visited or at Question Time after any speech I've made, has ever asked me what my own faith is. So if one looks at the matter from the point of view of the public interest, it's not just 'limited', it's almost nil. This is also true of the House of Commons itself. If you were to ask me what is the faith of a particular Member, I wouldn't be able to answer because I just don't know, and we don't ask each other, when we are expressing our views, on what basis these views are founded. As far as our political activities are concerned, I think that on the whole the public is not interested enough to the point of wanting to ask one a question or even write to one about it and say, 'Well, now, what are your views and to what do you attribute them?'

This leads me on to a further point. I believe there is a tremendous job to be done, in this country certainly, in explaining the basis of religious belief and, in particular, our own Christianity. It is said, of course, that the Church is losing its influence over our fellow citizens, and there is considerable evidence that in some respects this is true. I feel that so much of it is the result of, quite simply, a lack of explanation of the basic tenets of the faith and what is involved in Christianity and the various aspects of it. Very little now is taught in schools, and in the outside world it is very seldom that you find that those who are addressing us, from the point of view of Christianity, get down to the foundation of the faith and face up to the questions which people – especially of the younger generation – are asking as to the reasons for those tenets and the justification for them. I think, therefore, that there is a tremendous job to be done in, literally, spreading the Gospels if we are to regain the interest and the participation of so many of our fellow citizens.

How that is to be done is in the hands of those who are our leaders in the religious bodies and those in the media who convey their views or give them the opportunity themselves of conveying their views. But, to put it quite crudely, I think that from the pulpits we need to hear rather less about the political or economic problems of Sierra Leone, or anywhere else, and we do need to have much more of the argument about the basic characteristics of our faith.

I would now go further than that, and I would say that it is equally important that we should be given the chance to learn and understand about the fundamental factors in other beliefs. And here, I think, there is really an appalling ignorance. We ought to know, by the time we finish our schooling, what are the characteristics of the Muslim world, what are the characteristics of the Hindu world, what are the basics of the other faiths which exist in different parts of the world. We have to realise that we are really quite a small part of the world and that we have to create a relationship, not only in our religion but also in our political life and our business life and our social life, with those who have quite different faiths from our own. Let us remember, too, that the similarities between faiths can be surprisingly pronounced and the need for co-operation is absolutely essential if we are going to have a peaceful world, which we see even more desperately now we need, and if we are not going to have conflicts, as happened in past centuries, between those of different beliefs. This has been brought home to us, very strongly indeed, by the conflict in Yugoslavia, as well as by some of the civil wars in the former Soviet republics. So I want to emphasise how important it is that we should set out to learn about other faiths and compare them with our own and see where it is possible to co-operate with them.

When it comes to the question of Christian values and politics, I would say that it does depend upon each one of us in politics as to how we apply those Christian values. I find in all this time in the House of Commons that there are really comparatively few issues on which one has to sit back and say, 'Well, now, does this correspond with the values of my own faith?' By far the greater part of the decisions we reach, certainly in this House of Commons, are not controversial from the point of view of Christian beliefs, but there are some about which one has to make up one's mind as to whether one can support them ethically, or whether one should oppose them, or whether one can just abstain on them. They don't come very often, but when they do come, they are important. And I think here that one comes to another aspect of our tenets: that is, freedom. We do believe, as Christians, in the freedom of the individual to decide and to act or not to act. Now, this does mean that toleration is required. One has to recognise that other people of different beliefs, or even Christians with a different approach, have got the right to pursue their own course, and I, as a Member of Parliament, have not got the right to stop them doing so. It is at this point, I think, that difficulties can arise in political life, particularly on the matters affecting society as a whole. It is essential that we should recognise the importance of society in the Christian faith, and, as I have said, that does mean, in my view, the extension of toleration to a very great extent. Now, of course, there are some who don't agree with this and say, 'Oh, no, this cannot be tolerated.' Well, I'm sorry, but I differ from them, and I believe that the willingness to tolerate is essential for the development of co-operation in our world; and that co-operation is essential if we are to ensure a peaceful existence, which must always be one of our major objectives.

Indeed, it is only when a society is at ease with itself that you can have a peaceful and understanding existence, and this must be founded upon all groups in society being able to accept other people's views. I'm afraid that in this country, over the last fifteen years, we have a large part of the time not been at ease with ourselves. I am sad that is so, but I have to face up to it; and the consequence is that we have become, in my view, a very inward-looking society, a society which has lost confidence in itself, a rather selfish society. And as we are not at ease with ourselves, it means that we have to take it out on other people, sometimes through our internal affairs and sometimes through our external affairs. We have had too many examples of late of those in political positions taking it out on other people, particularly those abroad – foreigners and those in the European Union. This, I think, is both alarming and most undesirable. Too often in human affairs, people attack others because they are aware of their own vulnerability, or perhaps because they perceive a shadowy reflection in others of their own shortcomings. So it behoves us to become at ease with ourselves, and that does mean understanding and toleration of other people's views. I think this is very important from the point of view of our relations with people in other countries and in the handling of international affairs altogether. Of course, it is of prime importance so far as the European Union is concerned, our place in it and the influence we can have on it.

But I want to put that into context because ever since the end of the Second World War, for forty years or more, we had a position in which there were two dominant super-powers. It took them some time to work out how far each of them could go without causing disruption with the others. Each had their alliances and countries which supported them. But now all that's gone. With the collapse of the Soviet empire we have the United States as the sole remainder of the two. But I believe that we have now moved into an entirely different world, and it's a world of five powers, and this requires even greater understanding than in the past. And I'm afraid that at the moment a great deal of that understanding is lacking. When we just had the two super-powers, other countries that might have engaged in disputes did not do so because they were afraid, quite simply, that one of the super-powers would drop on them like a ton of bricks and they would suffer immeasurably. But all that has gone as well, and with the main exception of Vietnam in the post-war world we had vast areas of peace, and now we have considerable conflicts.

The question is how those should be handled. I come back to my point that it must be through understanding and toleration. And at times one sees today there is a grave danger of those elements being missing. If we take the five-power world, we have got the United States itself, and that country is finding it difficult to adjust itself to a position in which the other super-power has almost disappeared but others have now arisen in its place. It's finding it difficult to adjust itself to other people's beliefs and the actions which support them. It's finding it difficult to adjust itself in economic circumstances, to recognise the problems of other countries if they are going to be able to provide social justice for their people. It's finding it difficult always to adjust itself to the needs of the under-developed world.

But then we still have Russia with us – militarily a very powerful country but internally divided as never before since the Revolution. And it has many different faiths: it has to adjust to all of them, in particular to the Muslim faith. Then we have the People's Republic of China, now one and a quarter billion people. When I talked to Zhou En-lai about this in 1974 he promised me that the population wouldn't go above 900 million people, but now he has broken his promise and it will continue to increase. The country has developing resources but an entirely different institutional framework to that of Europe and North America. This itself produces problems, and we might just look at these for a moment.

Because of its past history, because of the various faiths which are there in a country which is well over two thousand years old in its organisation, because of the problems which it has faced from time to time from the outside world, it has got a different approach. And it is this which is not always understood by those in the West. I remember Deng Xiao-ping saying to me, 'Well, what sort of constitution would you produce for a country of one and a quarter billion people?' I couldn't tell him because no one had told me what to say, but it's always been in my mind that we say, 'You ought to have the same democratic system as we've got.' Well, how would we get on with one and a quarter billion people? We have quite a lot of trouble with 55 million, let alone one and a quarter billion. And this has to be taken into account when we are talking about human rights. And it is over this item that the problems are occurring more and more among the countries of the five-power world.

We then come to Japan – 120 million people – technologically the leaders of the world but very unified. They don't have problems of different faiths in Japan or different aspects of language. There is very little difference in the organisation of society. And so for them that is a simpler problem, but they still have the problem of the relationship with the other countries of the big five and particularly with the United States.

And then, as a fifth power, we have the European Union, of which we are a member. Of course, it may well be that in another twenty or thirty years India will join the five and become the sixth major power. Then again we will have the problems of the faith and the relationship of India with neighbouring countries and especially those with which it was at one time united under British rule.

Well, then, what do we have to do about this? I think we have to recognise that we cannot impose our faith and our beliefs on these other countries. We can try to persuade them by argument and discussion. I do not believe that we should try to impose our will on them by economic or other means. That is only going to cause great hardship to their people, great bitterness in their relations with other countries, particularly Europe and America, and will in no way help to solve the problems which I have already described exist between us. Now this affects particularly the Soviet Union and the People's Republic of China as well as Japan. If we say to them, 'You have got to do *this* about human rights or else we put an embargo on you,' that is not going to produce the result which we want, which is a peaceful world society with justice being done to all the peoples in it. That, I believe, is the Christian faith. There should be a peaceful system of co-operation and social justice for the peoples of all different countries.

When the United States sent its Secretary of State to Japan and said, 'You have to reach an agreement,' they said, 'Thank you very much, but we don't want one.' And so he had to go home.

When he went to Beijing he said, 'You will do what we tell you about human rights, or else you will not get into the GATT,' (as it then was, the General Agreement on Tariffs and Trade, and now is the World Trade Organisation). And they said the same thing: 'Thank you very much, but you'd better go home.'

Well then, the Secretary of Commerce arrived a month later and said, 'Forget all about that on human rights. I want a trade agreement with you.'

And they said, 'Very well. Here's a $5 billion trade agreement.'

So the first approach had no influence on them at all. The second approach gave them both what they wanted. But a third approach was lacking, which was to persuade them of the benefits of moving in the direction of human rights. They need to be persuaded of this and not threatened, and this applies also to a great number of the Middle Eastern countries, which have got completely different faiths from ours, different standards, and whose actions are very often completely unacceptable to us. Of course, what makes it even more difficult is that many of those countries whose judicial systems we couldn't support, and whose actions afterwards are not sustainable, are left unaffected, whereas others are taken in hand and various means, embargoes and so on, used to persuade them to change the course of their actions. This causes great trouble among these countries and does not help us to achieve our purpose.

I have emphasised the need to understand these problems, and we have now got a much better opportunity, provided that we know how to use it. I remember being in a command post in a hole in the ground in Normandy and listening to a very weak radio broadcast which quoted speeches which had been made in the election for Roosevelt, and the one that stuck in my mind was 'We are now one world – we are one world at war. Every country is now at war.' But they couldn't foresee that we would in fact, in less than half a century, become one world, if not entirely at peace, then predominantly so. And what I mean by that is that it doesn't matter whenever anything happens in the world, or wherever it is, within a few seconds it's on the radio and within a few minutes it's on television, and everybody can see it all over the world, and hear it all over the world, and so the whole of the world's population is experiencing exactly the same thing at the same moment.

This, therefore, has led to an infinite mass of information for our fellow citizens to digest. They are confronted with all these facts and these incidents. Many times these are unpleasant and, to put it quite bluntly, a large part of the world is learning for the first time what war is really like. They see what is happening in Yugoslavia. They've seen it in Somalia. They see it in other parts of Africa – in the utmost detail. Some of us, of course, have had that experience in person. But, as one veteran said to me the other day, 'You know, we never talked about these things. We never told our families about these things.' And I had a letter from the son of one of the former troop commanders in my regiment, saying, 'My father will never tell us anything about what he did while he was in your regiment. Can you send me a letter telling me all the details?', to which I had to reply, very politely, 'No, I'm afraid I can't. If your father doesn't want to tell you, I'm not going to tell you on behalf of your father.' But now, of course, this is all public knowledge and public sight, and they see what's been going on in Yugoslavia, and they are horrified, quite naturally, by it, but they don't realise that wars have been like this in the past and wars are very unpleasant things, and that is why someone like Yitzhak Rabin who had been involved in war did not want to show again what a splendid fighter he was but wanted a peaceful world. And that too is our ambition.

Now, Yugoslavia: how could that have been dealt with in our project of ensuring peace and social justice in that country? I discussed all of this with President Tito when he came to stay with me. I said, 'You're very healthy and active, but you are over eighty, and what's going to happen when you go?'

And he said, 'You have got nothing whatever to worry about. I've bound these countries so tightly together that they all believe in one Yugoslavia, and they will never break away.' Then he said, 'You look rather doubtful.'

I said, 'Well, I am doubtful, quite honestly.'

'The other thing,' he said, 'is that along our border we have Communist countries. We are never going to allow them to cross our border.'

I said, 'That is more convincing.'

He didn't foresee the collapse of the Soviet empire, which then led to the collapse of Yugoslavia and its breaking into war. That was a bad thing which came out of our talks. The good thing was that I learned that he never drank anything except whisky, and the only whisky he would ever drink was Chivas Regal, and so every year on his birthday I sent him a case of Chivas Regal, and this brought about very good international relations.

But if we're looking at this way of maintaining peace, then, of course, one's mind turns automatically to the United Nations, now celebrating its fiftieth anniversary. Was there any way in which we could have foreseen the outbreak of strife in Yugoslavia? Well, yes, there was. If the United

Nations had achieved its first purpose, when it was set up, of having information about the world, or the danger spots of the world, it could have seen that there was possible danger in Yugoslavia and it could have prepared for it.

Similarly, if we in Europe could have agreed upon a way of speaking with one voice on External Affairs, then we might have handled the Yugoslavia situation in a more circumspect, considered manner. But we had none of those things, and what went wrong was the German recognition of Croatia before anyone else really had the opportunity to consider the options – and so Croatia became an independent country. Then followed the movement of all the other parts of Yugoslavia, the complete break-up, and all the horrifying strife we have seen resulting from the sudden bursting of a dam of ancient and long-subdued racial and religious hatreds.

So there are lessons there for us in the international organisations. If we are going to achieve our purpose of peace and social justice, a single foreign policy, this also applies, of course, to the European Union. If we are going to be effective in maintaining peace and social justice, then we have to look to our external arrangements as well as to our internal ones. The external arrangements must mean that we have a common foreign policy and a common defence policy. It's the only thing which makes sense. A union which has fifteen countries really cannot carry on its world affairs, its international relationships, with fifteen different lots of arrangements. I'm afraid that we have not yet convinced this country, or its government, that this is the answer. 'Yes,' they say, 'perhaps we ought to have joint arrangements but not in Brussels. No. Separately.' But this is rather like saying here that of course we have got to have economic arrangements and tax arrangements; they can be in Westminster. But not foreign policy or defence policy. No, we'll put foreign policy in Liverpool because that's on the sea and is outward-looking and ships go to America and that sort of thing; and defence policy, we'll put that up with the Scots because they always like wars, and they can look after us in that respect. It makes no sense at all. If we're going to have plans to provide for peace, and prevent wars, then we've got to have a centralised organisation in which we play our part and we can exercise great influence. We have to recognise we are no longer a great empire. We must have an arrangement of co-operation and co-ordination, and that requires that it should be done for the European Union as a whole. So far as our social justice is concerned, the European Union must be able to work out what is required for the Union to be at ease with itself. That means we have to have a full and proper organisation for dealing together with all of these things.

We are a Union now, and that puts obligations on us as well as opportunities. We cannot expect to tell the remaining fourteen countries exactly what they've got to do. It does mean that each of us has to make sacrifices for the common good as well as take the benefits that are offered to us as individual countries, and that is the way in which in the European Union we can secure social justice. I am absolutely convinced that if we are to achieve our objectives of peaceful development and social justice, we have to recognise that both individuals and governments have a part to play. You cannot exclude governments from this. There are certain responsibilities which governments must assume, and they have the legislative and fiscal means to bring about social justice. That is one of their most important functions. As far as individuals are concerned, they must be given opportunities to develop for themselves, but also in the context of recognising the requirements and needs of their fellow citizens. The true foundation of a civilised society is a concept of personal responsibility. You cannot have social justice based on pure selfishness, and that is sometimes where we find ourselves now at a disadvantage. Individualism can be encouraged to too great an extent when it ignores the position and the future of its fellow citizens. It is all too apparent that economic growth alone cannot create a peaceful or a contented society. People need a sense of belonging as well – and they need a sense of security. That is the foundation of both British Conservatism and European Christian Democracy.

Very well, then, we now have a world position in which we have to adjust and in which we have to help other people to adjust. This is particularly true of helping the developing countries. I was a member of the Brandt Commission in 1979, and we put forward a world plan which would have made a great impact on the developing countries. Unfortunately, it was not accepted at that time, and although a meeting was called, in Mexico, President Reagan and Mrs Thatcher both strongly opposed it and refused to take any action about it. But these peoples, whom we have seen in so many places now, who are undergoing immense hunger and thirst, and whose living conditions are completely unacceptable, have not been given the assistance which they ought to have had and which would have enabled them to move closer to us. You can say that in Eastern Europe now we have an opportunity in the European Union to work together with developing countries. We ought to have a complete plan, part of which has already been worked by the European Union. It's not without its problems – let us not think that: if you take some of the countries of the East, formerly in the Soviet Union, their standard of living is only 20 per cent of what ours is here. Now, it is not easy to bridge that gap, and especially as we ourselves expect to be moving forward the whole time. They have not only got to catch up with the past but they have also got to catch up with what we are able to do in the future. But I think it is right, according to our belief and in the cause of social justice between nations and countries, that we should help them as much as we possibly can in order to bring about the improvement of their own situation.

This may seem to you like a big agenda – and it is. There are times when one would like to sit back and say, 'Well, in politics we have solved our problems, and people are happy. Now we can relax.' After forty-five years I have never found that to be the case, and I don't think it is going to be in the future; and I certainly cannot foresee a situation in which economic growth matches people's growing expectations. It's solving the problems and trying to achieve one's ends which give one the satisfaction, sometimes the excitement, and also enables one to know that one is trying to carry out the principles in which we believe and on which we have been brought up.

And so I would ask you, in all the work that you're doing – have been doing with the Cathedral in particular – to pursue these ends, to think carefully about the way in which our objectives can be met, to recognise that as far as our fellow citizens are concerned we have a great deal to do to explain to them the justification for our own faith and that, as far as other beliefs are concerned, we ought ourselves to master them and be able to understand them so that we can, where possible, co-operate with them and prevent the peace from being broken. We must also convince the rest of the world – in this new five-power world – to give up the idea that we want to impose a further colonial regime (which is what many of them think at the moment), and to believe that we want to co-operate with them as equals, colleagues and friends. Then they will realise that they can work with us when they come to understand us a little better. If we can start tackling all of those problems, and the Church can give us a lead, I think we shall have a much better chance in the next century of having a stable world, a peaceful world and a world in which social justice for our peoples prevails.